(Continued)

Envisioning Literature

LITERARY UNDERSTANDING AND LITERATURE INSTRUCTION

Judith A. Langer

International
Reading
Association

Teachers College
Columbia University
New York and London

Published simultaneously by Teachers College Press, 1234 Amsterdam Avenue, New York, NY 10027 and the International Reading Association, 800 Barksdale Rd., Newark, DE 19714

"Forgive My Guilt" by Robert P. Tristram Coffin reprinted with permission of Simon & Schuster, Inc., from *Selected Poems of Robert P. Tristram Coffin*. Copyright 1949 by Robert P. Tristram Coffin, renewed 1977 by Mary Alice Westcott and Robert P. Tristram Coffin, Jr.

Excerpt from "I See You Never" by Ray Bradbury reprinted by permission of Don Congdon Associates, Inc. Copyright © 1947, renewed 1974 by Ray Bradbury.

Excerpts from *Sky Dogs*, copyright © 1990 by Jane Yolen reprinted by permission of Harcourt Brace & Company. Reprinted in United Kingdom by permission of Curtis Brown Ltd.

Library of Congress Cataloging-in-Publication Data

Langer, Judith A.
    Envisioning literature : literary understanding and literature
    instruction / Judith A. Langer.
        p.   cm.—(Language and literacy series)
    Includes bibliographical references and index.
    ISBN 0-8077-3465-9 (alk. paper).—ISBN 0-8077-3464-0 (pbk. :
    alk. paper)
    1. Literature—Study and teaching—United States.   I. Title.
    II. Series: Language and literacy series (New York, N.Y.)
    LB1575.5.L25   1995
    372.64044—dc20   95-24278

ISBN 0-8077-3464-0 (paper)
ISBN 0-8077-3465-9 (cloth)
IRA Inventory Number 159

Printed on acid-free paper
Manufactured in the United States of America

02 01 00 99 98 97 96 95   8 7 6 5 4 3 2 1

Before all, a dedication:
For my mother,
who first invited me to enter
literary worlds

Contents

Preface

This book is about reading literature, thinking about it, and teaching it. Although literature is a central part of the school experience, its role in students' intellectual, social, and personal development is often underestimated. There is an implicit belief that literature education is a "good thing," but the contribution of literary understanding to human as well as intellectual development is largely ignored. Here, I offer a way to rethink the contribution of literature to intelligent thinking as well as its role in schooling. In the end, I hope that the ideas I discuss and the classrooms I describe will contribute toward a practical pedagogy—a way to rethink what it means to understand and learn literature, as well as ways to teach it. In doing so, I hope to explicate the role literature can play in students' cognitive, critical, and humanistic development.

To live through a literary experience involves exploring as fully as one's awareness permits, while maintaining an openness to future possibilities. Although such exploration is often associated with intuitive thinking, its role in sharp reasoning and critical understanding is less often recognized. In this book, I call upon a 7-year research project at the National Research Center on Literature Teaching and Learning to describe ways in which literary imagination can be used to explore options, solve problems, and understand others—a productive form of human reasoning that is useful not only in school but also at work and in everyday life. I draw my examples from a series of studies involving a collaboration among some 50 university researchers, teacher-researchers, and their students. They were critical to the development of the notions about literature education that I discuss in this book. Together, we explored our own thoughts, behaviors, and experiences when reading and discussing literature. We also explored ways in which we could create classrooms that were as provocative as possible, opening imaginations and exploring possibilities.

The teachers varied in experience, age, gender, and cultural background. They differed as individuals, with different personalities and teaching styles. They taught students in different grades and with different life stories. Their schools were in different types of neighborhoods, with different degrees of community support for change, and with different styles of school and district administration. The teachers used different books, and their students participated in different activities. Yet, with all these differences, there were some underlying assumptions that governed all the classes when the students were most involved—engaged in exploring horizons of possibilities, building envisionments, pursuing their inquiries into literature and life. These shared assumptions about teaching and learning literature provide the basis for this book.

This project could never have been completed without the professional interest and personal dedication of the collaborating teachers, their students, and the schools and districts in which they worked. They have taught me an enormous amount. I would also like to express my deep gratitude to the field researchers, for their hard work and expertise: Noreen Benton, Carla Confer, Phil Davis, Sr., Judith Dever, Roseli Ejzenberg, Ester Helmar-Salasoo, Elba Herrero, Irene Pompetti-Szul, Barbara Risalvato, Doralyn Roberts, Eija Rougle, John Sandman, Mary Sawyer, Francine Stayter, Mack Strahl, Fiona Thompson, Dee Warner, and Beth Weatherby. Their reports and analyses of classrooms in action contributed greatly to the ideas I discuss in this book.

Many people provided helpful feedback along the way. The comments and questions I received from colleagues in response to my talks and articles were extremely important to me; they challenged me to consider issues from other perspectives. I would like to thank Richard Beach, Courtney Cazden, George Hillocks, and Taffy Raphael for their helpful comments about particular reports along the way, and Elizabeth Close, Russel Durst, Anne McGill Franzen, Doralyn Roberts, and Eija Rougle for their thoughtful critique of my first draft of this book. Carole Saltz and Carol Collins, from Teachers College Press, were not only helpful in the preparation of the manuscript but also a delight to work with.

Many people at the National Research Center on Literature Teaching and Learning served as sounding boards, especially Arthur Applebee and Alan Purves. Genevieve Bronk managed the teacher research institutes and ensured that the project staff had the resources to carry out their work. Ellen Mainwaring organized our efforts and tried to meet our needs. My thanks to each of them.

A project of this magnitude could never have been undertaken without the willingness of the U.S. Department of Education and its staff at the Office of Educational Research and Improvement (OERI) to fund long-term efforts of this sort. The sustained funding permitted us to develop into an intellectual community and to engage in both theory building and action research, learning from the daily realities of living classrooms and creating a web of knowledge that only time, reflection, and sustained research could generate. Rita Foy, our project monitor, was incredibly supportive throughout. My deepest thanks to her and to the other OERI staff.

I would also like to express warmest thanks to the Rockefeller Foundation for supporting me as a resident scholar at its Villa Serbelloni in Bellagio, Italy. It was here that I retreated, in palatial solitude, to complete this book.

J.A.L.
Bellagio, Italy

Envisioning Literature

LITERARY UNDERSTANDING AND
LITERATURE INSTRUCTION

1

Literary Thought and Literate Mind

Through literature, students learn to explore possibilities and consider options for themselves and humankind. They come to find themselves, imagine others, value difference, and search for justice. They gain connectedness and seek vision. They become the literate thinkers we need to shape the decisions of tomorrow.

Literacy involves manipulation of the language and thought we engage in when we make sense and convey ideas in a variety of situations; it involves ways of thinking, which we learn in the many contexts of our lives. Such literacy fosters the personal empowerment that results when people use their literacy skills to think and rethink their understandings of texts, themselves, and the world. It gives importance to individuals and the oral and written texts they create and encounter; it calls upon and fosters the kinds of language and thought that mark good and sharp thinking. This is the kind of literacy that can underlie every aspect of literature education across the grades, empowering all students to reflect on and potentially reshape themselves and their world. We see it at work in the classrooms that follow.

THREE CLASSROOMS

Cyrus Ford and the students in his 11th-grade English class are reading the play *Marty*, by Paddy Chayefsky (1955/1983). After a few animated discussions, Cyrus asks the students to write about what the play means to them. Selected papers are read to the class by volunteers and serve as an impetus for discussion. Here are some examples:

> To me, the play says that you shouldn't let anyone decide who your friends are going to be, except you. I have learned from the characters that if you feel good about something and believe in it, then

1

you should go for it, and not let anyone or anything stand in your way.

In this play, I feel that some of the content has opened my eyes and heart. During parts of the play I began to think of times in my own life when I judged someone by the way they looked. It's not something done on purpose, it's just ignorance.

To me the play expresses the fact that no matter what people think, you have to follow your heart. And Marty is trying to make his life complete. His mother is beginning to worry about herself when Marty gets married, what is to become of her. At first I thought Marty would die an old lonely fat man. But it seems Marty is going to get married.

The readings were followed by a 2-day discussion about the students' interpretations of the play, its connection to their own lives and to those around them, its resonance with other pieces they had read, and its connection to life in general—to constraints and dreams, finding identities, and taking steps. There were difficult times, when students backed away from the discussion or changed topics. But they kept coming back. They were involved in developing their own interpretations and finding personal meaning. This is a rare event for "low-track" students in this economically and ethnically diverse school. At the beginning of the school year, most of the students would enter class, put their books on their desks, fold their arms on top of the books, and put their heads down. They would "turn off." Here they are involved and thoughtful participants as they engage in reading, writing, and discussion: not bad for students who "read" several years below level and are considered to have "attitude" as well as academic problems.

Now let's look at a discussion in Kendall Mason's 12th-grade Advanced Placement English class in a predominantly working-class community. The students are completing their discussion of the play *Antigone* by Sophocles (trans. 1984). They have been trying to understand why Antigone acted as she did, pondering her need to "fight for her brother's honor," her "loyalty to her family over the state." They continue their exploration:

REBA: It's a flaw in the eyes of the state, and that's what . . .
CARLA: That's what gets her.

REBA: It's ironic that her flaw is also a virtue. It's not her flaw, it's Creon's fault.

CARLA: No, it isn't her flaw because *flaw* is defined as what gets a tragic hero into the tragedy, and her loyalty to her family is what kills her in the end.

MR. MASON: Her loyalty or her willingness to push that loyalty against the state?

DAN: Arney was saying about how a lot of the things that ancient Greeks were teaching back centuries ago have no relevance in the 20th century. But there are many countries here today that don't practice things like democracy, and a lot of other views that ancient Greeks had.

ARNEY: That's totally irrelevant. I was saying of the interpretation. You have to look at the way they write and why they wrote them [the plays] back then. You didn't write them to say that, "Hey, we're all human, we're all dying" and everything. That's not how they wrote them. They wrote them to prove a point.

JESSE: Who are you to say how to interpret things?

ARNEY: Because that's what I and about all of us have learned throughout our lives.

MR. MASON: Terry?

TERRY: We thought it humanized her. And Arney attacked that. But, we supported that she was made to seem such a martyr, and so invincible to everything. And then she shows that she's weak and can't overcome everything. I think she would bury her brother, and everyone else too, but in this case she's emphasizing that with her brother, it was her last brother. If it was my kid. . . .

Preceding this discussion, the students had given their own dramatic reading of the play and had also engaged in several small group and whole class discussions. The students participated as they usually do, taking chances and probing meanings. Although *Antigone* is difficult for the students, Kendall encourages them to discuss, develop, explain, and defend their interpretations—and to compare them with one another's as well as with some writings by literary critics that he has duplicated for them to read.

Compare these classes with Tanya Weber's first-grade class in a suburban, largely professional community known for its excellent schools. Tanya reads to her class every day. The month is April, so they have already had many discussions about literature. Today, Tanya has just finished reading *Just a Dream* by Chris van Allsburg (1990).

Ms. WEBER: How do you feel right now, after hearing the story?

BOB: Sad, because he kind of, he might have a couple more garbage cans.

KEVIN: Like a time machine, because first he is at home.

Ms. WEBER: [unclear] time machine brings you to the future. Who agrees with Kevin? Let's talk to Kevin.

GREG: Like I was the boy in that time machine. He figured things can be better if

HEATHER: I agree with Kevin, because Chris van Allsburg put lots of details in it so you really feel you are the little boy, the character.

Ms. WEBER: Chris van Allsburg! Maybe he was writing about himself.

ASHLEY: How could his bed . . .

Ms. WEBER: Maybe it was a real dream.

LUCIEN: I agree with Kevin, because I really did feel I was in the story too. I was sort of the people, like saying stuff.

Ms. WEBER: Who were you in the story?

LUCIEN: The ducks.

Ms. WEBER: How did that feel?

LUCIEN: I missed the pond we used to have.

Ms. WEBER: How did you feel?

LUCIEN: Sort of sad that we were always going—other people [thinking] "We don't need this pond," and making a house on top of it.

Ms. WEBER: Oh boy, some people in the world say, "Who cares about a duck pond?"

LUCIEN: And maybe the boy was going to say this is the ducks' place to get some food. Maybe they were

JEANNE: trying to find the water.

Ms. WEBER: So, you agree with Lucien?

The discussion continued in a similar fashion, with the students agreeing and disagreeing with one another and using the literary discussion as an opportunity to develop their own understandings.

Despite the wide range of reading selections and very different sets of students involved, these literature lessons have much in common. The students in each of these classes feel like, act like, and *are* participants in a community of literate thinkers. They interiorize their various readings in a quest for personal meaning, examine the text and life to varying degrees from a critical perspective, and treat others' comments as having the potential to enrich (as well as challenge) their own understandings. They also know that they have the right to disagree, and that they are likely to modify if not change their ideas with time. And so it is with literature. Solitary thought continues, and more public discussion is always possible. In a literary experience there are no ends, only pauses—and future possibilities.

I have chosen these examples because they depict teachers who are trying to make substantive changes in how they teach and in what their students learn, and because they show students' responses to these attempts. They are typical of the kinds of experiences and interactions that permeate literature lessons where students' thinking is at the center of concern, where students are granted ownership for their own growing interpretations, and where they have practiced engaging in conversations about their growing understandings.

LITERATURE IN LIFE

Literature plays a critical role in our lives, often without our notice. It sets the scene for us to explore both ourselves and others, to define and redefine who we are, who we might become, and how the world might be. Writers as diverse as Wayne Booth (1988), Jerome Bruner (1990, 1992), and George Kelly (1955) suggest that stories provide us with ways not only to see ourselves but also to re-create ourselves. As we read and tell stories through the eyes of our imagined selves, our old selves gradually disappear from our recollections, our remembrances of yesterday become firmly rewritten, and our new selves take on a strength and permanence that we believe was and is who we are. All literature—the stories we read as well as those we tell—provides us with a way to imagine human potential. In its best sense, literature is intellectually provocative as well as humanizing, allowing us to use various angles of vision to examine thoughts, beliefs, and actions.

My claims for the personal, social, and intellectual benefits of literature should come as no surprise. Every reader of this book has experienced such connections with literature. Many philosophers, psychologists, and language scholars who have influenced education have made distinctions between not-literary and literary experience as reflecting two very different ways in which human beings go about thinking, relating to situations and ideas, and organizing their discourse (Barthes, 1986; Calvino, 1986; Harding, 1937). For example, Jerome Bruner (1986) speaks of paradigmatic and narrative modes of thought as providing distinctly different and complementary ways of viewing reality. He suggests that people come to fuller understandings when they use both, likening them to the ordered thinking of the scientist and the humanely inquisitive mind of the storyteller. James Britton (1970) makes similar distinctions in his work on the development of language abilities in a comparison between spectator and participant roles, as does Louise Rosenblatt (1978) when, in describing the reader's role, she contrasts efferent and aesthetic reading.

On the one hand, we can hold ideas and feelings outside ourselves— keeping them distant, objectifying them so that we can inspect them and relate them to other ideas and feelings and events and actions. From a distance, or in the paradigmatic role of the scientist, we can be dispassionate, logical; we can analyze and evaluate how things relate to one another and from that perspective see how they work. In *Mind*, Suzanne Langer (1967) calls this way of making sense *objective experience*. It involves a discursive way of reasoning that occurs when people treat meaning as if it were an object to be viewed and held apart, scrutinized with a keen and distant eye.

On the other hand, *subjective experience* occurs when we look within ourselves for meanings and understandings, when we bring new experiences and ideas closer to ourselves in ways that let us "see" them from the inside. Here, we gain a participant's perspective on what they look like, feel like, taste like, and how they relate to the ideas and feelings of other participants. We come to make sense and gain understanding through interiorizing, as does the storyteller.

Each type of experience, objective and subjective, treats meaning differently. As would be expected, then, we come away from each experience with somewhat different understandings. Say, for example, that you are taking piano lessons and want to play well. You might study sight reading and musical theory, do finger exercises, and practice a great deal. You might even tape-record your own playing in order to critique it. Over time, after acting on what you have learned from such objective experience, it is likely that your technique would improve. But what if you also immersed yourself in Alfred Brendel's or Richard Goode's playing of the Beethoven sonatas? You could let their music invade your senses and seduce you by their sounds, as their best playing can do. You not only hear the tones and phrasing but are also aroused by them; you sense the sounds *and* where they take you. By interiorizing their music, you respond to the musicians' particular interpretations. And if you put yourself in their places, you can even begin to sense the feel of their (your) fingers on the keys and the sounds in their (your) ears—the same, but different, heard through the filter of your own experience.

Through such subjective experience, you can live music from a number of vantage points. You might choose to hear music through an older classical pianist's ears, perhaps Vladimir Horowitz, or through the ears of such different composers as Bach and Stravinsky, or through the ears of a classically trained jazz musician-composer such as Wynton Marsalis.

The insights you gain from subjective experience can give you many new ways to develop your own playing. Objective and subjective experience are neither antagonistic nor exclusive; they go hand in hand. One focuses on personal meaning and experience, the other on the world outside yourself. Together, they invite a fuller and more complex understanding.

Imagine that you have been following the 20th-century debate about abortion. You can read and argue the issue on purely legal or religious grounds, developing logical and well-defended arguments from one perspective or the other. But stepping into the lives of the antagonists and imagining what motivated their opinions, or projecting how you, your neighbors, and those you love might be affected by one or another governmental ruling, could add sensitivity as well as complexity to your own understandings. It might even help you clarify your own position, with greater conviction. Objective and subjective experiences need not conflict with each other; instead, they provide different perspectives on the same phenomenon (in this case, the same conflict).

Every one of us engages in both objective and subjective experiences all the time; we use them to make sense and round out our understandings. Of particular importance, from my perspective, is the recognition of subjective experiences as a normal and natural part of understanding. Literature education has the potential to nurture and develop this critical ability, calling on its special power to draw the individual into the experience. For purposes of this book, it is not necessary to take on the problem of which texts are to be considered literary and which ones are not. Some theorists in English studies question the separation between literature and nonliterature (e.g., Barthes, 1967; Foucault, 1981; Derrida, 1980); certainly the definition of literature has changed over time (Reiss, 1992). Here, however, I focus on the kinds of thinking a person does when reading—any reading—not on the texts themselves. Although, as I have argued, subjective experiences are basic to all aspects of a thoughtful life, literature classes are the one place where such thinking can be systematically nurtured and developed throughout the school years.

THE DRAWING-IN POWER OF LITERATURE

Narrative, the form through which we most often experience subjective reality, calls upon, embodies, and *is* everyday human experience. We live and tell our lives through narrative. In doing so, we are faced with viewing a life—a human condition—in its entirety. In life, we cannot parcel out certain conditions and put others aside. History counts; there is desire and conflict; a variety of perspectives come into play. We need to deal with the many forces that create a living reality, including the inseparability of the parts, the gaps, the shifts in perspective and time, the multiple vantage points from which each situation can be viewed, and the many participating voices (Lauter, 1990; Ricoeur, 1980; Scholes, 1985). These disturbing and sometimes antagonistic features come together at one point—the intersection of our sensibility (life experiences) with those conditions created during our transaction with the literary work (Rosenblatt, 1978). It is here that we not only learn to see things from many perspectives but also become aware that there are many possibilities, many truths, and no final resolutions. In all likelihood, there is something yet to come. Tempting as it might be to seek objectivity, in a sense, this is impossible.

When we read Alice Walker's *Possessing the Secret of Joy* (1992), we cannot do a purely Marxist interpretation of female circumcision as it is practiced in parts of Africa, shutting out other kinds of considerations that might come to mind. To do so would require shutting out some of the pain and suffering she depicts and force us to hold the realities (hers and our own) apart—to create an objective rather than subjective experience. To live through a literary experience, in both a cognitive and a humane sense, requires that we see it in as much of its totality as our awareness permits.

It is this openness that invites the imagination. From the perspective I have been discussing, imagination becomes a way to look beyond things as they are and seek new and potentially enriching perspectives (Egan & Nadaner, 1988; Greene, 1988; Warnock, 1976). It permits us to create new combinations, alternatives, and possibilities, to understand characters and situations in ways not necessarily suggested when we take things as they are. It permits us to become fuller, more thoughtful, and more informed members of this world—in both literature and life. It becomes an essential part of how we reason and understand.

2

Building Envisionments

In the last chapter, I began to describe the complexity of the text-worlds in people's minds when they engage in the literary experience. How do these text-worlds develop? In the most direct explanation, they grow from people's active quest for sense as they read. Barthes (1977) calls this the "passion du sens," the passion for meaning. This is where the concept of envisionment becomes central.

I use the word *envisionment* to refer to the world of understanding a person has at any point in time.[1] Envisionments are text-worlds in the mind, and they differ from individual to individual. They are a function of one's personal and cultural experiences, one's relationship to the current experience, what one knows, how one feels, and what one is after. Envisionments are dynamic sets of related ideas, images, questions, disagreements, anticipations, arguments, and hunches that fill the mind during every reading, writing, speaking, or other experience when one gains, expresses, and shares thoughts and understandings. Each envisionment includes what the individual does and does not understand, as well as any momentary suppositions about how the whole will unfold, and any reactions to it. An envisionment is always either in a state of change or available for and open to change. This act of change is "envisionment building." Envisionment building is not just a literary activity; we build envisionments all the time when we make sense of ourselves, of others, and of the world.

For example, when you meet someone for the first time, let's say at a party, you might have no knowledge of that person except for physical appearance, dress, and an assumption that the individual is acquainted in some way with the person who is giving the party. With even these first few clues, you begin to build an envisionment of the person (more or less detailed, depending on your interest). You know that the person is a woman, middle-aged (looks about 45), well dressed, and wearing what seem to be expensive clothing and jewelry; all in very good taste, if a bit formal. Her reserved manner suggests that she is a private person, perhaps a bit withdrawn. She looks and sounds well educated and professional but is somehow different from the professorial types who are at the party. And so it is that you build an envisionment of who she is. At first your envisionment is filled with a few knowns, some maybes, and a lot of questions (I know she's well dressed. Maybe she's new here. Can she be a relative or friend from out of town? Perhaps she's the computer analyst I've heard my friend talk about). And so continues the internal conversation, the envisionment building.

The word *envisionment* refers to the understanding a student (or teacher) has about a text, whether it is being read, written, discussed, or tested. Such envisionments are subject to change at any time as ideas unfold and new ideas come to mind.

During reading, for example, envisionments change with time; as more of the selection is read, some ideas are no longer important, some are added, and some are reinterpreted. Even after the last word has been read and the book closed, the reader is left with an envisionment that is subject to change. Changes can occur through writing, additional thought, other reading, or class discussion. Envisionments grow and change and become enriched over time, with thought and experience.

INTERACTING WITH TEXTS

Consider Jim, a seventh grader. Both Jim and his teacher consider him to be an "average" student. He seems happy at school, participates in class discussions and school projects, and is well liked by his classmates and teachers. He says that he likes his English class (which is activity- and reader-based), but sometimes finds reading in his other classes "hard" or "boring." Although students in his English class are encouraged to self-select many of the pieces they read, he prefers to read at home because, "Then I read what I like." He likes sports magazines. Jim says that he also likes to read poems and to write them. In poetry, "The author is trying to make a point and I like to try to see what he says."

Against this backdrop, let us look at Jim's reading of "Forgive My Guilt," a poem about hunting by Robert P. Tristram Coffin (1949/1966). For this reading, Jim is doing a think-aloud, voicing his thoughts aloud while reading the poem. Jim's interspersed comments follow the lines of the poem, just as they did in his reading.

Forgive My Guilt

[Maybe someone has probably done something
wrong, or once, like, maybe someone wants to
apologize for doing something wrong.]

Not always sure what things called sins may be, [This person might not,
doesn't know what a sin is or doesn't know when he's done a sin
maybe, or has sinned.]

I am sure of one sin I have done. [She didn't know she had sinned.]

It was years ago [maybe it was when this person was little] *and I was a
boy,* [Yep, this person was little when this sin happened.]

I lay in the frostflowers with a gun, [This person might have shot something, or, why would a little boy be with a gun? I don't understand. I mean if it's like a pellet gun or something, but not (unclear) or anything. I don't understand why he would have a
gun.]

The air ran blue as the flowers, [they were blue flowers] *I held my breath.*
[Maybe he wanted to, like, shoot a bird or didn't want to scare it
away.]

*Two birds on golden legs slim as dream things ran like quicksilver on the
golden sand,* [Yep, he probably wanted to shoot birds, with maybe
a pellet gun or something, some sort.]

My gun went off, they ran with broken wings [He must have shot one or
both of them, with broken wings they couldn't fly.]

Into the sea, [he must have been at the beach] *I ran to fetch them in* [I
guess he went and got them. Maybe he wanted to treat them, you
know, to help them get better, and maybe he was, like, sad 'cause
he did shoot the birds.]

But they swam with their heads high out to sea, [They ran away. They were
scared, the birds didn't know why he was running towards them.
The birds might have thought, they might have thought that he's
done enough damage, why come and get me.]

They cried like two sorrowful high flutes,

With jagged ivory bones where wings should be. [The birds were in pain,
in agony, and they were in pain.]

For days I heard them when I walked that headland [The birds, there must
have been a lot of birds there, crying when he walked on that
beach, or he was near a body of water.]

Crying out to their kind in the blue, [They must have probably been in
the water. Maybe the birds, when they were crying.]

The other plovers were going over south [Must have been in the winter,
    'cause birds go south when it's cold.]
On silver wings these broken two. [Maybe they had broken wings, the
    birds.]
The cries went out one day; [he heard all the birds crying] *but I still hear
    them* [He hears the birds crying.]
Over all the sounds of sorrow in war or peace [Maybe he doesn't know
    why he shot a bird, why he wanted to, what led him to shoot the
    bird. Now, 'cause he's holding it in forever.]
I ever have heard, time cannot drown them, [He doesn't think that birds
    won't die of old age or something.]
Those slender flutes of sorrow never cease. [I don't understand what cease
    means.]
Two airy things denied the air!
I never knew how their lives at last were spilt, [He must have, like, killed,
    hurt the bird and maybe the bird never got well or anything, and
    the bird might have died because it got shot.]
But I have hoped for years all that is wild, [He won't, maybe he never
    tries to kill anything else in his life.]
Airy, and beautiful will forgive my guilt. [The birds will never forgive.]

A bit later, I return to Jim's thoughts as captured in this transcript.
For now, we can see that as he reads, he is connecting the poem with his
life's experiences and knowledge as well as the text-world he is developing—he is making initial sense of the poem. When asked at the end
of his reading what this piece meant to him, Jim answered, "It's about
sin. About how you sin so easily, without even knowing it." At the beginning, Jim's think-aloud revealed that he already had a clue that the
poem might have this meaning for him. He picked up on this at the end,
noting, "After the first sentence . . . , he [the narrator] said he didn't know
what sin was, and the title gave like a little hint. Because someone didn't
forgive him, I guess I said [thought] in the beginning." But as Jim read
on, he decided that the poem was about self-imposed rather than external blame. In retrospect, he said, "Like now he's older, but he knows.
When he was little, he didn't really. It seems like he didn't really care.
But now he does."

Similar to our process of building an envisionment of a new acquaintance at a party, Jim is in the process of creating his understanding of
the poem. He begins with few clues but gathers them into a sensible, if
sparse, envisionment for the moment. With time, as he reads on, his ideas
round out; they change and shift. New and richer and potentially different understandings are before him; his focus is on the future. He also

knows that the changes in his envisionment are a combination of his own experiences and what the poem says.

Jim's poem (his understanding of it) is a function of his life, his experiences, and his values. He knows that people are not the same and that interpretations can differ. Jim lives in a suburban community bordering a large rural area. He has gone hunting himself and has many classmates who hunt for sport with their families. He knows that some of his classmates might not come away with his interpretation of the poem. They might say, as Jim explained, "'Yeah, like wow, he shot a bird.' That's it. . . . Like they just wouldn't care about the bird. 'Oh, there's one out of a million birds.'" He also thinks that the poem can be interpreted in yet another way. "It can be, I mean, how a bird grows and gets shot and dies. I mean there goes his whole life from one little pellet." But he thinks that the poem is more about how the person feels; it is the sense of remorse that Jim comes to interiorize over time through his changing envisionment.

Like Jim, a reader experiences many changes in envisionment when interacting with any particular text. The envisionment changes as the text progresses and understandings shift. New problems, feelings, and occurrences within a work bring new thoughts and suppositions to mind. Gaps in the work, shifts in vantage point brought about through dialogue, the constant reorientation of time and perspective invite us to muster all we know from life, fiction, and fantasy to build understandings and suppositions—to build upon an ever-changing envisionment.

Take, for example, *Beloved* by Toni Morrison (1987). The story immediately carries us into the life of Sethe, the central character; beginning with the first few words, we sense her deep sorrow. Baby Scuggs, Sethe's mother-in-law, is dead, and her sons Howard and Bulgar have run off. Only 10-year-old Denver remains with her mother. A flashback takes us into their home when they all still lived with Sethe at #124. The family's sadness is likely to fill our minds, and we wonder who they are and how this came to be. As we read on, the description of the dead baby's spirit provides us with only the scantest hint of the tragedy that will later unfold, yet it invites us to speculate about both the spiritual and the physical dimensions of intense grief. The literal meanings and actual discussions between Sethe and her old friend Paul D (they had both been slaves at the Sweet Home plantation) transport us into the tragedy, permitting us to read through the eyes of several characters, from differing vantage points. We begin to experience their horrors, feel their terrors, and build a growing understanding of who they have come to be. These initial realizations, powerful as they are, are merely a hint of what we will learn—the torments Sethe lives with and the pain that shrouds everyone she knows. With time, through Sethe's tale, we build envisionments of the inhumane treatment she and the others have endured and the sense of futility that pervades their lives.

The earlier chapters provide us with hints as to why the baby's spirit has invaded Sethe's house, as well as Sethe's willingness to let it do so. Our envisionments fill with speculations, and as the story continues, some details of our earlier envisionments are likely to be dropped (such as descriptions of Howard and Bulgar) and some added (such as what life at Sweet Home was like, why and how they fled the plantation, how Sethe's baby died, and how the name Beloved came to be). With each additional image or idea, our envisionments change, becoming more complex as a sense of Sethe's tragic life and the lives of those around her unfolds in our minds.

We can think of envisionment building as an activity in sense making, where meanings change and shift and grow as a mind creates its understanding of a work. There is a constant interaction (or transaction, as Louise Rosenblatt [1978] calls it) between the person and the piece, and the particular meaning that is created represents a unique meeting of the two. An envisionment isn't merely visual, nor is it always a language experience. Rather, the envisionment encompasses what an individual thinks, feels, and senses—sometimes knowingly, often tacitly, as she or he builds an understanding.

But what happens across time that causes our envisionments to change? As we read, we develop new thoughts. Some earlier ideas, questions, and hunches no longer seem important or pertinent to our understanding. For example, we begin to understand some of the family's experiences when we read about the circumstances surrounding Howard and Bulgar's flight from home, develop some hunches about why they do not keep in touch, and wonder what might happen to them. However, they do not remain at the center of our envisionments for long. It is through the later tales of indignity upon sorrow that we come to realize the immensity of the terror, grief, and love that is embodied in Sethe, and we develop a growing awareness that the baby's spirit represents one more tragedy with which she must contend.

From this perspective, an envisionment represents the total understanding a reader has at any point in time, resulting from the ongoing transaction between self and text. During the reading of any particular book or play or chapter, a reader has a "local" envisionment, which changes as new thoughts (from the work, from the reader, and from other people and events) lead to changes in overall understanding. In this way, a local envisionment evolves into a "final" envisionment that is not the sum total of what we thought along the way but is a modified envisionment resulting from all the transmutations of local envisionments that have led to this one. Some ideas from local envisionments remain in the final envisionment, but other parts are gone—no longer critical to the meaning of the piece. Each local envisionment is qualitatively different from the one it replaces; it is not a tree trunk with layers of its past within it but rather a butterfly that is essentially unique in each new stage of life. Even after the last word is read (or the final scene completed and the curtain drawn), we are left with an envisionment that is also subject to change with additional thought, reading, discussion, writing, and living.

The notion of envisionment leads us to assume that after a reading, all students (and the teacher as well) have their own "initial impressions" that are subject to change in response to their own and others' ideas. It also suggests that reading is an interpretive act (in the meaning-building sense used by educators, not in the sense of formal interpretation discussed by literary critics). This process of interpretation is essentially social, involving a person's mind in the intertextual web of personal history and experience that Bakhtin (1981) speaks of—the texts and subtexts (and pretexts) of one's past, one's responses at the moment, and the texts that will be generated or encountered in the future. Such interpretation does not necessarily involve "hard work," nor is it necessarily academic. Envisionments develop and change all the time, even when we are curled up with a mystery or reading a romance (Radway, 1984).

STANCES DURING ENVISIONMENT BUILDING

Let us consider ways in which envisionments develop—the kinds of knowledge students might call upon as they make sense. This will help us gain a better sense of ways to support them in their efforts. From the very start, understanding *is* interpretation, and people have a number of options available as they develop their interpretations. These options— I call them "stances"—are crucial to the act of envisionment building, because each one offers a different vantage point from which to gain ideas.

The stances are not linear; they have the potential to recur at any point in the reading and result from varying interactions between a particular reader and a particular text. Thus, stances are part of every reader's envisionment-building experience, but the particular patterns they follow and the particular content they contain are based on a particular reader's experiences and expectations while transacting with a particular text.[2] I have identified four such vantage points. I briefly describe each and give examples from students' think-alouds; then I examine a class discussion to demonstrate ways in which the stances develop and interact during everyday classroom talk.

Stance 1: Being Out and Stepping into an Envisionment

When we begin to read, we are out and stepping into an envisionment. We try to gather enough ideas to gain a sense of what the work will be about (as in real life, when we try to pull together as many ideas as possible about a new acquaintance). Although fragile, it is a place to begin a conversation with ourselves—in the real world or in text-worlds. Because there is little to build on (because we are "outside" an envisionment), we pick up any clues that are available and try to make sense of them in terms of the little we already know. We search for as many clues as possible, but the meanings we seek (and derive) are usually superficial; the search is for breadth rather than depth.

In this stance, we generally begin to develop envisionments by using our knowledge and experiences, surface features of the text, and any other available clues. Particularly when the reading has just begun, we use this broad search in order to form initial ideas and suppositions about the characters, plot, setting, situation—and how they interrelate. However, "being out and stepping into an envisionment" occurs throughout a reading, not only at the beginning, when ideas are new. Even after the envisionment has been built, it is possible to become derailed from it. This can happen when the vocabulary is unfamiliar, or when a sufficiently unforeseen and inexplicable event causes us to become puzzled and lose focus. Even at the end of a piece, we can become derailed from an envisionment by a surprise ending. In each case, we search for starting places to rebuild the envisionment, in ways that are essentially similar to the earlier idea-gathering stage.

We have already seen Jim trying to step into an envisionment at the beginning of "Forgive My Guilt," when upon reading the title he says,

> Maybe someone has probably done something wrong, or once, like, maybe someone wants to apologize for doing something wrong.

Later, he speculates about the narrator's age,

> Maybe it was when this person was little. . . . Yep, this person was little when this sin happened.

In each case, his speculations grew out of the clues he was able to muster very early in his reading.

Stance 2: Being In and Moving Through an Envisionment

From these kinds of surface ideas (sometimes just a few are sufficient) and more experience with life or text, we become more immersed in developing understandings; we use personal knowledge, the text, and the context to furnish ideas and spark our thinking. In this stance, we are immersed in our text-worlds. We take new information and immediately use it to go beyond what we already understand—asking questions about motives, feelings, causes, interrelationships, and implications. This is the time when meaning begets meaning; we are caught up in the narrative of a story or the sense or feel of a poem. In this stance, we call upon our knowledge of the text, ourselves, others, life, and the world to elaborate upon and make connections among our thoughts, move understandings along, and fill out our shifting sense of what the piece is about.

Jim gives evidence that he is in and moving through an envisionment when, during his reading of "Forgive My Guilt," he says,

Yep, he probably wanted to shoot birds, with maybe a pellet gun or something. . . . Or both of them with broken wings and they couldn't fly. . . . I guess he went and got them. Maybe he wanted to treat them, you know, to help them get better. And maybe he was, like, sad 'cause he did shoot the birds.

Here, as throughout the reading, he speculates about what things "might" mean. He is trying and testing ideas and keeping his envisionment open to change. In this stance, he is building and rounding out meaning, using his momentary understandings to contribute to an evolving understanding of the entire piece. We see this later in his reading, when Jim says,

Maybe he doesn't know why he shot a bird. Now he's holding it in forever.

Stance 3: Stepping Out and Rethinking What One Knows

This stance is essentially different from the others. In all the other stances, we use our knowledge and experiences in order to make sense of the text-worlds we are developing; they are essentially envisionment-building stances. In this stance, things are just the reverse; here we use our developing understandings, our text-worlds, in order to add to our own knowledge and experiences. It is the time when the thoughts in our envisionments give us cause to shift the focus of meaning development for a moment, from the text-world we are creating to what those ideas mean for our own lives.

We engage in this stance when *Beloved* causes us to reflect on our own feelings about subjugation, slavery, and power and we realize how shallow these might have been once we experience them through the perspective of Sethe, Baby Scuggs, Paul D, or Denver. Here we use our envisionments to reflect on something we knew or did or felt before having read the text. Thus we see the reciprocity between our fictive and real worlds: the envisionment illuminates (and influences) life, and life illuminates (and influences) the envisionment.

As we read, this "stepping back and rethinking what one knows" does not occur as frequently as the other stances. This is partly because all works do not intersect our lives in ways that we can necessarily reflect on and learn from, and partly because it may take time and cumulative literary experiences before works have an impact on us. However, because this stance is so powerful and eventually pervasive, its potential impact is a primary reason that we read and study literature—to help us sort out our own lives. As readers, we know that the lessons of literature can be a valued aspect of the experience. They provide us with a set of mirrors in which to view our possible as well as our present selves. They also help us reconsider what we have done and imagine alternative values, beliefs, and emotions. We see Jim in this situation as he discusses his thoughts about sin after his reading of "Forgive My Guilt." He philosophizes about guilt and aging:

> I understand about sin and all, but, I mean, why would you hold on to it for so long? Just let it out now. . . . 'Cause, I mean if you do it, you're probably when you're little. It's probably better to tell, like not holding it in for so long.

Stance 4: Stepping Out and Objectifying the Experience

In this fourth stance, we distance ourselves from the envisionment we have developed and reflect back on it. It is here that we objectify our understandings, our reading experience, and the work itself. We reflect on, analyze, and judge them and relate them to other works and experiences. It is in this stance that we can focus on the author's craft, on the text's structure, and on literary elements and allusions. We can also become aware of why a particular author or piece holds significance for us, whether and why we agree with others' interpretations or don't. In this stance we become critics, aware of tensions between the author's and our own sense of the world, aware of insinuations of conflict and power, and aware of critical and intellectual traditions and the place of this work within them.

In all, this is a stance that involves seeing text and meaning at a distance, permitting (but not requiring) a more analytical look. We "step out and objectify the experience" when we find ourselves comparing *Beloved* to, say, Ralph Ellison's *The Invisible Man* (1972), whether looking more closely at the characters' life situations and histories or reading against the text from the perspective of race or gender. We also step out to objectify the text when we recognize or are reminded of a biblical or mythic allusion—such as when Beloved emerges whole, thirsty, and new from the water, or when we contemplate the trials Sethe must face—and bring new depth of understanding to our reading as a result of connecting those allusions to our own growing envisionments. We are also in this stance when we judge (or prejudge) a work or focus on how it is put together. Jim did this when he was trying to figure out why he liked "Forgive My Guilt":

> This one [poem] makes sense to something, about someone's fear of something, what they think of something. . . . A children's poem would be you know walk, talk, rhyming words. But this is someone's feelings, about something. . . . I've never really heard a poem about sin. It's like one of a kind.

As I mentioned earlier, the four stances do not occur in a linear sequence; they can occur and recur at any time during the reading, during later discussion or writing, and during later reflection on the work. Over time (and clearly this can be an extended experience), we weave a growing web of understanding. Our envisionments develop through the shifting relationships between self and text that occur from stance to stance. The stances offer variety to the kinds of meanings we consider, filtering our thoughts through slightly different vectors as we develop our understandings of the text, our envisionment, and life.

In the first two stances, our thoughts are on our envisionments themselves. In the third stance, our thoughts are on our experience and knowledge in the real world. In the fourth stance, we objectify our envisionments, holding them apart for inspection. The stances serve as a way to think about the same general issue in different ways. In the first stance, we gather initial ideas; in the second, we are immersed in our text-worlds; in the third, we gain insights from our envisionments; and in the last, we reflect on what it all means, how it works, and why.

A CLASSROOM EXAMPLE

This notion of envisionment is particularly important for instruction. It provides a way to conceptualize how to help students think about ideas, consider alternative views, modify and defend the more salient ones, clarify and distinguish their responses from others', and build interpretations—in other words, to become more thoughtful readers. Because the stances represent the options readers use when they make sense, they can help us understand how we can provide instructional support that will help students think more clearly or effectively about the ideas they are considering.

Let us take a class discussion as an example. Barbara Furst always encourages her students to become members of a literary "community," discussing their understandings and concerns and reaching beyond. This lesson is part of a continuing class discussion of "Charles" by Shirley Jackson (1976). In the story, Laurie is a little boy who goes off to kindergarten and comes home daily with tales of the classroom rascal, Charles. His parents are fascinated with the escapades their child regales them with. However, at a parent-teacher tea, Laurie's mother learns from the teacher that there is no Charles in the class. We pick up on the students' third day of discussion, beginning with Dawn in her seventh-grade class:

> I still don't think Laurie is making Charles up. I'm still gonna say Laurie is Charles, because in the first line, I don't have my . . . [book], but it says something like, "I watched my sweet boy nursery tot to be replaced by a long-trousered character." It's shown, his mother thinks Laurie's behavior has really changed. In that first line, that line like sort of says like he was a really sweet little boy but then he got to kindergarten he wanted to grow up like fast. He was being different.

Here, Dawn is "stepping out and objectifying the experience." She focuses on the text for this moment (rather than the envisionment in her mind), using it as a way to explain or defend her understanding. The lesson continues:

Ms. Furst: Attitude was changing.
Annie: I think maybe he was trying to test his parents, because they never told him all that was bad, or Charles shouldn't do stuff like that. They just said what happened to Charles and what Charles did.

Annie is "being in and moving through an envisionment," as she is working through her understanding of what actually happened in school and why Laurie kept relating things to his parents.

Ms. Furst: Oh, that was a bad thing for Charles. They just kind of
    laughed at what Charles did. I'm surprised I haven't heard from
    you guys. Well, let's hear it. Greg?
Greg: I want to know what time period it is.
Other students: Yeah.

Here, Greg and the other students are "being out and stepping into an envisionment," in that they think it necessary to get some idea of the time in which the story takes place in order to better understand Laurie's stories and his reasons for telling them. The students then go on to discuss the time period, using the fact that Laurie wore blue jeans as evidence of recency. (Not unlike our own data gathering at the party.) The students then use time as a way to explore Laurie's story of Charles being spanked by his teacher and ask whether this would even be possible in schools today. Through this discussion, the students move primarily between the second and fourth stances, occasionally entering the first (when their argument breaks down). In this particular discussion, they do not enter the third stance—there is no evidence that their own knowledge or attitudes change. They recall and discuss their own related experiences with spanking and relate it to time because, as Greg says,

Well, I think the time is important because, I think if we were to
    solve the thing—Is Charles Laurie and is Laurie Charles, or is he
    made up—then I think we do need to really understand, try to
    figure out what time it is. Because, like Jonas says, wasn't there like
    a spanking rule?

The students' goal in this part of the discussion is to explore whether Charles is Laurie, and to do this, Greg (and most of the other students) think that it is necessary to figure out the era in which the story takes place. To do this, the students call on the knowledge sources that will help them most: their own related experiences examined against the text (stance 4). They then try out their ideas within their changing envisionments (stance 2), exploring, stretching, and reflecting.

The notion of stances provides us with a way to conceptualize a seamless process that occurs when students develop understandings. I do not mean to suggest that there is a fixed order in which these stances occur. Although it takes space and time to discuss the stances in a printed book that is itself linear, I use the term *stances* to refer to a recursive, mobile, and sometimes co-occurring set of strategies. And in some readings, a stance might not be called upon at all. Use of a stance varies, for example, based on a reader's familiarity with the content, structure, and language of a text; perceptions of the reading environment; and familiarity with the options themselves. Nor do I mean to suggest that people do or should call upon the stances in equal amounts—either within or across readings; in fact, the opposite is the case. The most frequently entered stance for almost all readers almost all the time is the second, where people are actively engaged in developing understandings, whatever their ideas might be. Only when a piece is extremely difficult (so difficult that meanings just can't get going or keep getting derailed) is the first stance used often.

I also do not mean to suggest that the stances be taught or tested separately; they are used by particular people at particular times when contemplating and developing particular text-worlds for themselves and are meaningful only in the collective ideas they allow a person to gather. Why do I bother to separate them and speak of them at all, then? Because the notion of stances and how they support an individual's understandings permits us to think about ways to enter a dialogue with students, asking them about their envisionments and some of the ideas they might contain. Such questions have the potential to open a dialogue in ways that validate students' own rich thinking, while helping them explore extended meanings. An understanding of stances can also help teachers conceptualize activities around literature and questions about literature that are thought provoking in a grand sense, that invite students to move in and out of the variety of stances as ways to consider and share their growing understandings.

In literary experiences, as students move among the stances, imagining is an essential part of meaning creation; it is a critical way in which students reach toward meaning and come to understand. The act of melding and exploring is at the heart of coming to know in literature, making it a powerful way of thinking about the options that are available to each individual and the futures that can be imagined. I discuss this issue of a literary orientation toward meaning in the next chapter.

NOTES

1. I was first introduced to the word *envisionment* when I worked on a test comprehension project in 1980 with Charles Fillmore and Paul Kay (Fillmore, 1981; Kay, 1987). Fillmore said that he had heard John Sealy Brown use the

term in a discussion of active thought during debugging in mathematics. Susanne Langer's (1942) "envisagements" are related. These early introductions to the notion of meaning change within the mind led me to develop the concept in ways that might be useful for learning and instruction. See, for example, J. A. Langer, 1985, 1986, 1987a, 1987b, 1990; Langer, Bartolome, Lucas, & Vasquez, 1990.

2. My conception of stances grew from a series of studies I undertook to better understand how students build envisionments when they read for literary purposes. Over a number of years, I studied students' participation in regular classwork and also their think-aloud comments as they read selected works. Since my first report of the work (J. A. Langer, 1990), the particular stances have been interpreted and used in ways that sometimes differ somewhat from my original, in particular by the National Assessment of Educational Progress (1990, 1992, 1995), whose reading framework was developed by a large community of scholars and practitioners who adapted the theory to suit the demands of a particular testing purpose.

3

The Nature of Literary Experience

The notion of stances leads us to another important aspect of envision-ing literature: the nature of the literary experience itself. What is it that differentiates the ways we come to understand when we engage in a literary experience (an essentially interiorized experience) from the ways in which we understand when, say, the major focus is discursive (pri-marily objective)? In real life, people become involved in literary ways of thinking in a variety of settings and for a variety of personal, recre-ational, and institutional purposes. People are affected by many frames of reference and can choose to locate themselves within a broad set of purposes and activities based on what they wish to say or do. These frames of reference are created in response to the social uses to which literary understanding may be put by particular people in particular situations, cultures, and subcultures.

For instance, hearing bedtime stories or grandma's tales of long ago, reading adolescent literature or Bible stories, watching New Wave per-formance art or performing it, and writing an autobiographical sketch or keeping a diary all have the potential to involve interiorizing. Since these experiences all occur in real-life social settings, they also involve the participating individuals in a complex web of human relationships. Personal feelings, associations, and interactions with others in the group invariably create a layer of motives that sit alongside the more obvious and general features of the activity. The many general uses for literate thinking and the more personal motives that underlie them are reflected in the everyday social environments in which we all live.

ORIENTATIONS TOWARD MEANING

Within these highly complex social settings there are two major forms of extended discourse that affect how our thoughts evolve. (These grow from the social context: What people around us are thinking about and doing and how we are interacting with them often affect how we organize or represent what we think and know. Our cultural and group affiliations and histories as well as our own personal identities also affect the ways in which we frame our ideas.) Alone and with others, people generally form their discourse either to create imaginary worlds or to make points. By this, I mean that people approach meaning in essentially different ways when their reasons for reading, writing, or discussing are primarily to experience (to live through the situation in a subjective manner), as opposed to when their primary goal is discursive (to gain or share ideas or information).

I am not suggesting that people become so driven by purpose that they shut out alternative ways of thinking. Instead, I am suggesting that in every language experience there is a more or less tacit and more or less compelling primary focus that grows from the individual (influenced by a large social construct of concerns, experiences, and traditions)—a focus that is essentially more subjective or one that is essentially more discursive. It grows from a person's primary purpose for thinking about or doing whatever it is she or he is thinking or doing. Of course, when we are engaged in an activity, we shift in and out of both modes of thinking, but our overall envisionment building is guided by our primary focus. Some people (e.g., Harris, 1988) question the notion of dominant purpose, suggesting instead a multiplicity of purposes. Although I agree that a person often has multiple reasons for engaging in any particular reading or writing activity, I contend that one holds more sway at any particular moment, even though it may later shift.

In both literary and discursive experiences, the meanings we develop are guided by our sense of the nature of the whole—in reading, a sense of whether the piece is primarily discursive or primarily literary. We have a sense of the momentary envisionments we are building at that moment, and also a sense of the overall purpose that causes us, from the very beginning, to orient ourselves in particular ways. Our expectations about the kinds of meanings we will eventually come away with vary, depending on whether we perceive our purposes as literary or discursive.

As I indicated in the first chapter, educators' approach to students' thinking has been surprisingly unidimensional; the focus has been on logical, discursive approaches to understanding. Educators have developed a language to talk about scientific or logical thinking, and a variety of instructional techniques have been generated from a wide range of theoretical paradigms that suggest ways to recognize, teach, and test such thinking. Not so for literary thinking. More attention needs to be paid to literary thinking, but not in the way that advocates a "cookbook" approach—the very idea of recipes is antithetical to this way of thinking. New understandings that can be incorporated into our more general notions of teaching would be much more useful.

As I will demonstrate later (and as I have already suggested), people don't enter literary orientations only when they read literature, nor discursive orientations only in science and social studies classes. And most often, we don't "select" an orientation. Instead, the primary orientation we engage in is socially situated; it isn't the orientation that is our focus, but the particular social activity. For example, when we curl up in a lounge chair with a best-selling novel, we tacitly expect to enter a literary orientation. And when we sit in the same chair with a newspaper or professional journal, we more likely expect to engage in a discursive experience. These expectations are related to the reasons we selected those particular pieces in the first place. To begin the discussion, I describe the general ways in which people make sense in each of these situations.

Exploring Horizons of Possibilities

I characterize the way our minds work when we are engaged in a literary experience as reaching toward a horizon of possibilities. Our reading proceeds at two levels at the same time, as if we were simultaneously rubbing our stomachs and patting our heads; our momentary understandings and our sense of the whole are both in a state of change. Our local envisionments and what they contain are influenced by our sense of the developing whole, but we also use our developing envisionments to reconsider the whole. Thus a literary orientation is one essentially of exploration, where uncertainty, and hence openness, is a normal part of the response and newfound possibilities provoke other possibilities. We consider feelings, intentions, and implications in our quest for the "real" story; we often create scenarios as a means of exploration.

This happens in real life all the time. For example, at the imagined dinner party, you learn that your new acquaintance is the cousin of a friend and that she is considering moving across the country to your city. You immediately begin to contemplate her motives and her situation. You wonder whether she is looking for a new job (perhaps she's lost the one she has; or maybe she's a climber, looking for a better job; or perhaps there's a significant other in her life who lives in town). Each possibility leads to yet another possible shape for the whole, as well as yet another local possibility to explore for the moment.

I selected the term *exploring possibilities* to highlight that the literary experience involves openness and inquiry—where we continually "try out" possibilities for the moment and for the future. And I selected the term *horizon* to remind us of the essential indeterminateness of the literary experience, that in literature there is no end; we cannot step closer. Instead, with each new possibility, our perspective changes and the horizon shifts, remaining elusive, just beyond our grasp.

One Reader. As an example, let us look at some excerpts from Jim's reading of the short story "I See You Never" by Ray Bradbury (1973). It is about a man, living in California, who is about to be deported to Mexico. Jim is the same seventh grader whose reading of the poem "Forgive My Guilt" I discussed in Chapter 2. (Throughout, I draw examples from a few of the many teachers and students whose experiences formed the basis of this book, to help you get to know them in a variety of their own contexts.) To understand Jim's responses, some information about his background might be helpful. Throughout his life, Jim has lived in a middle-class suburban community. It is bounded by poor rural and city areas whose residents have a variety of cultural backgrounds and incomes.

> *I See You Never*. [Sort of sounds, like, it could be about never seeing someone again, or something, like, someone passed away.]

At the beginning, Jim uses the title as a place to begin to build an envisionment, however tentative. Even as he gathers his initial envisionment-building clues, he speculates about the possibilities, and with the speculation, the horizons (the possible shapes for the whole) shift too. He goes on to read the story.

> *The soft knock came at the kitchen door*, [someone was knocking at the kitchen door—maybe it was a neighbor of this person] *and when Mrs. O'Brian opened it*, [it must have been Mrs. O'Brian's neighbor] *there on the back porch were her best tenant, Mr. Ramsey [Ramirez] and two police officers, one on each side of him. Mr. Ramsey just stood there, walled in and small*. [I'm not, I don't really understand what they mean by walled in and small. So Mr. Ramsey, I guess, was the tenant.] *"Why Mr. Ramsey," said Mrs. O'Brian*, [Mrs. O'Brian may be saying like, what happened. Why did you do this? How could you get arrested? You're my best tenant, maybe she's thinking.]

Here, we see Jim, already involved in the story and developing his envisionment, stepping into Mrs. O'Brian's shoes, imagining the situa-

tion from her perspective. Although he has read newspaper articles and
engaged in class discussions about Latino immigration and illegal aliens,
Jim has had almost no opportunity to meet bilingual speakers from any
Latino group. Thus, although he seems to understand Mr. Ramirez's
situation, he does not seem at all aware of the likelihood that the person's
name is not Mr. Ramsey, as he misread it, but one that is of Hispanic
origin.

> *Mr. Ramsey was overcome. He did not seem to have the words to explain.*
> [What happened? Why did he get arrested? Why did the police
> officer bring him home?] *He had arrived at Mrs. O'Brian's rooming
> house more than two years earlier and had lived there ever since.* [Mrs.
> O'Brian I guess runs, like, for people, maybe, like, they can't, like,
> maybe afford a real apartment, and they she gets a lot of people
> and they work and their paycheck goes into her fund, and they buy
> their food, and, like, so they might share this house or building.]

Jim still doesn't understand the living situation and is using something
he saw on television about group welfare homes to help him explore
possibilities. He realizes that this is speculation and easily considers it;
just as easily, he later drops it for another possibility that may be more
consistent with his growing envisionment. He reads on:

> *He had come by bus from Mexico City to San Diego and had then gone up
> to Los Angeles.* [Maybe he went up to Los Angeles to try to get rich
> or something. Like, maybe he tried to get a job up there.] *There he
> had found the clean little room with glossy blue linoleum and pictures of
> calendars on the flowered walls and Mrs. O'Brian as the strict but kindly
> landlady.* [Mrs. O'Brian maybe just took him in 'cause maybe he
> didn't have any money, and maybe she was, like, sad or some-
> thing.]

The next part of the story tells a bit about Mr. Ramirez's life in Los
Angeles and Mrs. O'Brian's pie baking. Jim explores their relationship:

> Did Mrs. O'Brian like this man, or was she just kind to him? Were
> they good friends or had something going like, I'm not sure about it
> yet, about what's going on between these two. Maybe they're just
> like tenant and like, maybe they're like friends, really good friends.

A bit later, we see that his earlier speculation about the group housing
has changed, and his sense of the whole with it.

Mrs. O'Brian I think is pretty mad at him. She did, like, let him rent the apartment and he is one of her best tenants.

Jim continues to explore possibilities when he later reads:

"I have been here thirty months," said Mr. Ramsey quietly, looking at Mrs. O'Brian's plump hands. "That's six months too long," said one policeman. "He only had a temporary visa. We've just got around to looking for him." [Oh, maybe he was an immigrant, like, he got away from Mexico, and he tried to have a good life here.]

Jim continues his reading, speculating about the events and emotions from the perspectives of the various characters as well as from his own. He uses his knowledge of life and feeling to imagine and empathize with the situation, to "root" for a happy solution. He also examines the characters' motives when he doesn't feel comfortable with their behaviors. When Mr. Ramsey leaves with the police, Jim is disappointed with Mrs. O'Brian's quiet acceptance, saying:

Well maybe she was emotional but just didn't want to show, she just didn't, she just didn't want to get too close to Mr. Ramsey. But then she did and she got so close that she was like real sad that he went away, that he got deported.

Throughout his reading of the piece, Jim keeps his options open, letting his explorations lead him toward empathy and understanding in an open field of possibilities.

Experiencing Literature. Like Jim, we explore horizons of possibilities, involving a melding of literature in life and life in literature. We use knowledge of the real and the imaginary as well as previous experiences with other literature as the basis for our explorations. We use what we have gathered from life and literature to explore emotions, relationships, motives, and reactions, calling on what we know or imagine it is to be (or not to be) human.

For example, in our initial reading of *Romeo and Juliet*, we might begin exploring how the story could unfold if the lovers' parents took the time to understand the depth of the relationship between them. This begins to shape a new understanding for the entire play (a new horizon). And then, as we read on, we might begin to question whether Romeo and Juliet are almost invisible characters, caught in a grand cultural feud. Perhaps even their parents are pawns in that feud, with the lovers' destiny beyond their parents' control.

Even when we finish reading, we continue to rethink our interpretations, perhaps at different times taking different approaches—psychological, political, mythic—toward the characters' feelings and actions. Throughout the reading (and our "reading" may get put aside and taken up again at different times), our ideas constantly shift and swell. Possibilities arise and multiple interpretations come to mind (prompted, perhaps, by our own musings, others' comments, or events in life). We also think beyond the particular situation, using our envisionments to reflect on our own lives, the lives of others, and conditions of the world in general. And so we expand our breadth of understanding, leaving room for alternative interpretations, critical readings, changing points of view, complex characterizations, and unresolved questions.

Maintaining a Point of Reference

The way we approach understanding and build envisionments is very different when we are in a situation in which we wish to gain or share ideas or information. It is the way in which we treat the whole that distinguishes the two. I characterize the discursive orientation as maintaining a point of reference. When reading primarily for ideas or information, we try, early on, to get a sense of the topic we are reading about or the point of the argument. This topic or point becomes our sense of the whole. Then, as we read on, we develop agreements, disagreements, and questions in relation to this point of reference.

Once we form a sense of the whole, we use new ideas to clarify our sense of the whole but rarely change it. Although we revise a local envisionment readily, it takes a good deal of countervailing evidence before we rethink and actually revise our sense of the topic or point. Let us look at Jim's reading of a science article, "Birth of the Moon" by Shira Birnbaum (1986), as an example. He is just beginning the piece.

> *Birth of the Moon. A planet the size of Mars comes hurtling through space at 25,000 miles an hour and smashes into the earth.* [Maybe a lot of people died, because if it did, I don't think that something would crash into the Earth. There would have been, I mean, how could a planet of some sort travel 25,000 miles an hour and smash into the Earth? I don't understand how that could ever happen.] *The planets explode at more than 10,000 degrees (Fahrenheit).* [It had to be boiling hot. Very hot.] *Earth is blasted out of shape.* [The Earth must not have been around any more.] *Rocks vaporize. And a jet of hot gas squirts violently into outer space.* [It must have been sort of, like, even though it says (unclear) but what kind? I don't mean, like, I'm

trying to say, hot water, maybe of some sort like that.] *A bright hot flash lights up our solar system.* [They must be talking about the sun or the moon. The title says, *Birth of the Moon.* I think it's probably the moon that's lighting it up.] *The moon is born.* [Okay, I was right, it was about the moon.]

At this early point in the reading, Jim seeks and decides on the topic of the article—the moon. Unlike his speculations when reading the title of "I See You Never," he uses his sense of the topic, the moon, to shape his search for more specific information. After reading about the impactor theory, his comments suggest that he is working toward building his understanding. He says, "Maybe like the moon formed from the Earth, from the Earth, and it was like it just broke off from the Earth." Still later in the reading, he struggles when some of the new information seems inconsistent with his understanding.

> So alright, maybe the moon broke off or, yes, I don't understand. I don't know why or how they could still have the same exact rocks and not maybe come off each other. But if they (astronomers) got samples from other places and it had the same thing, maybe they could have, like, all, kind of all been like a big ball and all broke off into these pieces.

Later on in the reading he says, "Well, I think I was right, because they did break off." Throughout his reading, he uses his decision that the piece is about the moon to guide what he considers and to determine how the parts relate to one another and how they contribute to his growing understanding of the moon's birth.

Unlike literary orientations, where horizons are always ready to shift, here the end is steady. It is foreseen and maintained, and the local envisionments and what they contain are developed in relation to the sense of the whole. This is not an inflexible sort of thinking: our sense of the whole can and does change. But this occurs only when a substantial amount of countervailing information leads us to rethink our general sense of what the piece or point is about. Otherwise, maintaining a point of reference serves as a guide, keeping our inquiry within bounds that are relevant. We refer our local envisionments back to our sense of the whole, checking to see that they make sense. This leads us to a more logical and concomitantly less open treatment of the whole.

I am not suggesting that questions and explorations do not occur in point of reference thinking. They do, but they are constrained by the point rather than opened by the horizons. Rather than asking questions to sustain ever-elusive horizons, we ask questions in our attempt to narrow the gap between what we know or don't know, what we accept or reject about the point of reference. We move toward closure.

One might argue that science is always open to new interpretations and that scientific reasoning is, in its own way, always relative, and I would fully agree. For example, scientific thinking is said to involve setting a hypothesis, which acts as a point of reference. Throughout an experiment or the working through of a proof, this hypothesis guides the individual's focus. Although the result of that inquiry might lead to yet another hypothesis, the questions are, in a sense, serial; thinking is focused within a series of successive explorations. In each exploration, the ideas we think about are guided by our overall sense of the topic or point. In a discursive experience, we use this topic or slant as a relatively steady reference point, and what we consider within our local envision-ment is guided and shaped by this sense of the whole. As our envision-ment unfolds, we use this sense as a focal point around which to orga-nize our growing understandings.

As I indicated in the first chapter, both approaches to understanding—maintaining a point of reference and exploring a horizon of possibili-ties—are essential to effective and intelligent thinking. Sometimes we call primarily on one, at other times primarily on the other. In most instances, they interplay in subtle but important ways, adding to and enriching our envisionments—affecting what we think, understand, tol-erate, and believe.

SOME CLASSROOM EXAMPLES

If we look back at Jim's reading of "Forgive My Guilt" in Chapter 2, we see that he was engaged primarily in exploring horizons of possibilities. He built his envisionment by considering how the boy-grown-to-man felt and feels, as well as how the birds might feel. And he related these to his sense of sin and guilt and growing up. These explorations led to shifts in his envisionment. By contrast, the students in the excerpt from Barbara Furst's class were specifically considering the issue of the era in which the story took place. This notion of era served as a point of reference for this segment of their discussion, which was shaped around this topic. Although the students widened their explanation of the rela-tionship between Charles and Laurie—returning to exploring horizons of possibilities—this portion of their discussion had a discursive orien-tation. Many rich classroom discussions move back and forth between the two approaches.

A First-Grade Class

A look at Tanya Weber's first-grade class provides a sense of how literary orientations are invited, possibilities explored, and envisionments
developed during class time. Here, discussion is an integral part of teaching, a way to get more deeply into a story and understand it better. In
the discussion, we see the students weave a web into an imaginary (and
interiorized) world. They connect and link stories they know to those
they are hearing for the first time, using them to extend their envisionments. The following example comes from a discussion of *Greyling* by
Jane Yolen (1991), a story of metamorphosis in which a fisherman finds
a bundle consisting of a little boy who later turns into a seal.

STEVE: I wonder why [unclear] in the water. Because he is so big
      enough, he's like 13 or 14 and he can go in the water.
Ms. WEBER: Moses [a boy in the class] just can't imagine why he can't
      go into the water now.
SCOTT: He can't go in the water for his parents don't realize—he's a
      regular boy now. If he goes into the water then he will be a
      bigger seal and turn back into a boy.
JESSICA: Maybe the water and when he [unclear] mother and father.
STEVE: Ah, if he goes in the water he turn into a seal. You know how
      the other boy was. There was little the mother and father prob-
      ably would think that he ran away. He ran away because like
      people said, I don't think they were wrong. Like Moses, because
      if he goes out, ah, like he did on that rock, he didn't change back.
      He didn't change into a human being. I think someone has to as,
      their home with a mother and father would be thinking that
      anyway, because they already told him 100 times that he couldn't
      go into the water.

The students are developing their envisionments as they explore horizons of possibilities: they are using their imaginations to create scenarios
as ways to help them try out possible understandings of the characters
and their reasons for behaving as they do. Moses continues this exploration, introducing the idea of a costume, trying out a possible scenario,
and then rejecting it:

MOSES: A seal costume, and then he throwed it away, and it landed on
      that rock because he was a—when the ah, part of our [unclear]
      human being. But, I don't think that happened. I think it was a
      costume and he had a zipper on his head or something like that.

In these excerpts, the first-graders are building their envisionments as they move through the possibilities of the story (stance 2). They move between real and imaginary worlds to gather and explore possibilities and develop their understandings of the story.

A 12th-Grade Class

At the other end of the grade span is Maura Smythe's 12th-grade class discussing *Sula*, another novel by Toni Morrison (1974), and developing their own envisionments as they interact (again in stance 2). Kara is in the middle of a presentation of the ideas she and her partner have put together on the characters and their motives:

CANDY: Nel is more calm with relationships and that Sula liked more like raunchiness and craziness, and with death, maybe that's the same as their feeling, like Sula likes death to be more exotic and different, like a different type of death, like burning. Where Nel, even with relationships, like the calm where he just sank and never came up.

Ms. SMYTHE: Um, I mean, I guess I was thinking, I don't know whether anyone else read this, like they were feeling guilty for saving them. Is saving Chicken Little part of this?

SUKE: For *not* saving him.

Ms. SMYTHE: Yeah, *not* saving him. In other words, when they're talking about, I mean, that's the part that's so confusing to me. Here they are watching. I mean, why would anyone feel content to watch someone drown?

KARA: Well, I think Sula panicked.

CANDY: Sula was more worried about it than Nel was.

KARA: Right.

CANDY: Sula was the one who ran into Shadrack.

KARA: And that was the only death that Sula was almost caught up over, and the biggest thing that struck her was the part with Shadrack, where he said always. That was the trivial part of the whole thing. That is forever on her mind.

Ms. SMYTHE: But why is she so upset about it?

KARA: About Shadrack?

Ms. SMYTHE: No, about, I mean, you said that Sula always reacts violently, and this is the last time she does?

KARA: No, I thought it was probably the, there wasn't a violent reaction, so it didn't give her the contentment that it gave Nel.

Ms. SMYTHE: Maybe I'm asking about Nel—content.

KARA: Well, it says that, I mean, Sula's dying says (*reading*)

> *Nel, she remembered, always thrived on a crisis. The closed space in the*
> *water; Hannah's funeral. Nel was the best. When Sula imitated her, or*
> *tried to, those long years ago, it always ended up in some action*
> *noteworthy not for its coolness but mostly for its being bizarre. The one*
> *time she tried to protect Nel, she had cut off her own finger tip and*
> *earned not Nel's gratitude, but disgust.*

So, that's kinda going back to, there's a couple of quotes of the trivial and the crisis. I don't know how that relates to human relationships in the entire picture.

MS. SMYTHE: I think I follow what you're saying, but I thought it was, I don't know, it's maybe we need, *I* need to talk more about why they don't do something about Chicken Little and does that have anything to do with, I mean, I thought Nel would feel content because she's got things under control. You know what I mean, like, if there's some big problem and she knows how to solve it. But watching someone drown isn't solving a problem. You follow what I'm saying? I'm not asking the right question.

ABIGAIL: Everyone has a different reaction to it [death]. Some people go crazy and start crying and screaming, and some people just sit there and are logical about it.

Here the students are exploring possibilities, considering and reconsidering motives and behaviors from the perspectives of the various characters as well as their own. Maura believes that this type of discussion gives her students a chance to build envisionments in a literary manner, exploring horizons of possibilities and leaving room for multiple interpretations. During an after-class interview about his perceptions of Ms. Smythe's teaching goals, Miles, one of her students, said, "Today was a good example. I don't think she wants to finalize there's a certain right or wrong. . . . She lets us decide what we think. I think that's fine. People are going to see things differently . . . and as I grow older, if I read it again, I will probably see things differently."

This sense of exploring local possibilities, often through considering meanings from multiple perspectives, leads students like Miles to expect this type of thinking to occur as a matter of course in discussions of literature, and to continue even after the discussion has ended. And therein lies the difference between literary and discursive approaches. As Maxine Greene (1995) suggests, in literary experiences, "we are not only lurched out of the familiar and the taken-for-granted, but we may discover new avenues for action. We may experience a sudden sense of new possibilities and thus new beginnings" (p. 379). Literature invites speculation instead of closure, leaving the reader with an envisionment examined, yet necessarily incomplete.

LIFE AND THOUGHT

I have tried to provide a sense of the nature of envisionment building and the ways this occurs when people are engaged in a literary experience. Before closing this chapter, I need to emphasize that if we were to chart the paths that different students took in envisionment building in response to any particular text, we would see many differences. Students' envisionments are affected by their differing experiences, their purposes for reading, their assumptions about what the teacher wants, and their perceptions of what is politically or socially correct.

Both the approach to reasoning and the content considered are affected by who the student is and how the student interacts in a particular social setting. Thus, in a real sense, every envisionment-building experience is different: for different people in the same situation, for the same person in different situations, and for the same person in the same situation at another point in time. But this does not mean that envisionment building is totally idiosyncratic or that "anything goes." The text's contribution to the meanings a person forms cannot be ignored. People from fields as diverse as linguistics (Pratt, 1976), literary theory (Booth, 1988; Iser, 1974), and philosophy (Grice, 1975; Searle, 1969) concur. Although we as readers play a major role in the meanings we orchestrate, the text (and the author behind it) influences our reading. There is a craft to writing, and every piece conveys ideas through a host of semiotic signs and signals. These serve as guideposts to evoke the ideas and images we choose to form, resist, or refigure. There is a tension in the relationship between text and reader, as well as variability from reader to reader; there is a fragile and ever-changing line between a sound (or probably sound) idiosyncratic envisionment and one that has drifted into a netherworld in which the literary experience itself is lost. For education, this does not mean anarchy but rather that the markers we use to help us recognize effective reading need to take individual readers and their own lives and thoughts into account.

The notion of envisionment building, with the concomitant stances and orientations that affect it, allows us to think of understanding as fluid and social. Envisionments are inextricably influenced by interactions and experiences in the classroom as well as outside of it. They provide us with a window into students' reasoning. They invite us to reflect on students' ideas, to enter into and support their conversations, and to provide them with a mirror to reflect on their own growing ideas. When classroom interactions are not sanitized (see Delpit, 1988; Dyson, 1994), the focus shifts not merely from text to students but from text to the people in a class—their histories, relationships, and personal identities. Students' entry into a classroom literary community offers them opportunities to explore assumptions, negotiate ideas, and imagine the possible—but more of this in later chapters.

I have developed the notions of envisionment building and literary understanding in an attempt to "unpack" the literary experience, to describe its essential qualities: what makes it uniquely valuable, and why literary studies have survived as a cornerstone of the curriculum. Although the literary orientation is not entered solely when reading literature (nor is it the sole orientation we use when reading literature), literature education is the main course of study in which students can systematically practice and develop proficiency in such thinking. Horizons-of-possibilities thinking is the special purview of the English language arts curriculum. The implications are great, providing a way to rethink what counts as knowing and what this means for instruction. In the next chapter, we begin to explore what all this means in the classroom.

4

The Classroom as a Social Setting
for Envisionment Building

The concept of envisionment requires us to regard the student as an independent thinker who is strongly influenced by group membership and history. In daily life, individuals exist, act, and learn both as members of various out-of-school groups to which they feel connected and as members of their school and class community. These multiple and sometimes overlapping selves accompany students through the schoolhouse door, making themselves known at various times, in various ways. Teachers are, in a sense, always outsiders to students' other worlds. But through literary experience, teachers can help students become aware of and use their various cultural selves to make connections, explore relationships, examine conflicts, and search for understandings through the literature they read and the interactions they have.

In the envisionment-building classroom, everyone assumes that each individual has a complex social identity as well as personal interests and concerns, and that a person's understandings are necessarily affected by the many groups and subgroups with whom she or he associates and identifies. It is also taken for granted that individuals will attribute different meanings to the works they read, and that to rob them of these differences would involve rendering them invisible. It would make them less rather than more able to construct their own envisionments and interpretations and to stimulate the thoughts of others.

Each member of the class is a learner about many things at many levels, and a teacher as well. Some are learning better strategies for making sense when they read, some are learning how to sustain discussion and examine an issue, and some are learning to consider points of view that are not their own. Further, some are learning to muster a tighter argument for their interpretations, some are learning to read against the text, and some are learning to consider issues of history and culture in relation to behavior. To make a class work, it is necessary for students to voice concerns that others might or might not share, identify points of conflict and explore them from many perspectives, and push their own and others' thinking along. For teachers, this means that we need to see the classroom community as a dynamic entity, changing and flexing in response to the individuals who constitute it.

The ways in which students use literature, their reasons for doing so, and the kinds of meanings they expect to derive from their experiences depend on history and context (see, e.g., Gates, 1992). Each student is a complex individual belonging to any number of subcultures that can be identified by shared beliefs, mores, and ways of communicating and behaving. Because of its particular confluence of social, historical, and cultural differences, each group has a potential to treat literature in somewhat different ways (see, e.g., Bloome & Egan-Robertson, 1993; Dyson, 1994; Lauter, 1990; Minnick, 1990). The home can be considered one such subculture, the neighborhood may or may not be considered another, the place of worship still another, friends another, and the various classes at school still others. Some of these subcultures may overlap, and a student may join new ones at any time. In becoming a member of any particular subgroup, an individual learns group-appropriate ways to participate.

For some students, the local place of worship is a central context for using literature: Religious stories, prayers, and hymns may be read, memorized, interpreted, or embellished, depending on the particular community. Most students also have a family context for using literature that might involve sharing and discussing a range of literature from print and media, the telling of family or ancestral stories, the spinning of life's narratives, and so on. And these literature experiences might involve retelling, memorizing, interpreting, or embellishing, depending on particular family traditions. Students also have friends with whom they watch videotapes and television programs, read fiction, create song lyrics, play computer adventure games, act in a drama club, or share favorite magazines. These activities, too, might involve differing amounts of interaction and thoughtfulness, depending on the traditions of the particular group (Heath, 1983; Wolf & Heath, 1993).

These limited examples make the point that most individuals have a variety of experiences with literature, experiences that engage them in a variety of ways of thinking. Any theory of literary understanding must encompass this variety, focusing on students as individual human beings who are also members of various social and cultural groups, coming together as participants within the classroom community. Such a community involves tensions and balances between personal identity and group affiliation, individuality and connectedness. Recognition of these

tensions and balances between individual and group helps us conceptualize and support the most effective learning and teaching.

WHAT LITERARY DISCUSSIONS LOOK LIKE

The goal is to help students become involved in literary discussions that
are real—that share the social features and patterns of thoughtfulness
that are evidenced when "real" people discuss literature in everyday
life outside of traditional classroom contexts. To help us reflect on how
such communities work, let us look at a group of adult readers discussing
"The Story of an Hour" by Kate Chopin (1984). This is a very short story
of a woman who is told that her husband has been involved in a fatal
train crash while away on a business trip. After receiving warm con-
dolences, she retires to her bedroom, where she is consumed with unexpected feelings of freedom and promise. After relishing her imaginings
for some time, she is called downstairs to greet her husband, who had
taken another train. She dies of heart failure.

As they finish reading the piece, some people laugh self-consciously
and groan.

JANE: I had read it before, but I had forgotten the ending. And then I
    just, it was too much to bear. She thought she was free. Didn't
    even know that maybe she wanted that . . . and now all of a
    sudden here she is. A joke.
CORA: I remember reading it before, and just dying at the end, when
    her sister was, "Open up, don't be so sad." and she's in there just
    rejoicing and looking out the window, la, la, la. And seeing him, I
    just thought, oh no, the poor thing, she was free, and now, the
    irony. Just unbelievable. I toyed with teaching it to my class, and
    I thought, Oh God, would they appreciate this? Yesterday life
    was long, today it's not long enough. Wonderful story.
DIANA: I was thinking [that] the positive and negative is always
    within all of us, and we don't always look at parts of that.
    Usually the negative. And if we're really honest with ourselves,
    there are those things about our marriages or whatever, our
    relationships, that are
Jane: I know. The thought probably did go through my mind. I
    wonder if . . .
DIANA: And you don't know. You don't know how you would feel.
CORA: It reminded me of a couple of other stories I read. One was a
    Doris Lessing one, "Room 19," and "Yellow Wallpaper" or

something, where the women *are* going crazy. And even another one of hers [Chopin's], *The Awakening*, where they are inside themselves, going crazy with oppression or repression, in their own little world, in their own little families. And this one, "Room 19," the woman goes to this hotel every day. She has rented a room and just stays in there, like just screaming and going crazy, and her husband doesn't know why, or whatever, and it goes on and on like that. And that's what it reminded me of. Women's thoughts and thinking and when everybody and their family thought they were happy and they did for all of the children this and that. They're going out and just for a few hours in the afternoon, freaking out somewhere. That's what it reminded me of.

SONJA: A kind of feminist way. That's too bad. Again, a woman lost. Too bad for her.

TOM [the only man in the group that day]: As I started reading it, I looked at the author. I had never read anything by her. And then, as I read this story, I began to try to place, I was trying to figure out where this sort of, where you know, the setting, the, I didn't catch on to the husband's friend, Richard's the name. Richards, I thought, seemed very English, and then after on, later in the story, I think I began [unclear] Victorian era, England, possibly might be my guess as the setting of the story. And then what surprised me was the dates, her dates [1851–1904] and the writing of this particular story in relation to women's literature of today.

BARBARA: That was interesting.

OTHERS: Yeah.

CORA: That someone like that, maybe a century ago. . . . And it's wonderful. And her book, *The Awakening*, is a small volume, and she's American. And when it was published, I mean, it was the story of this woman just awakening, and just, "Oh my God, what is this trap that I'm in?" But it was set back in the late 1800s. Oh my God, and it was just radical, revolutionary, and banned in a lot of places, and just if you read that. I mean women couldn't read it. They were tucking it under the bed, this and that.

Here we see individuals voicing their initial thoughts about the piece, ideas growing from the envisionments they had constructed by the time they had finished reading. But almost immediately, the discussion engages them in new ideas, and they begin to respond to one another and comment on ideas that they may or may not have thought about earlier. Jane is the initiator who gets things started, in a way freeing others to speak. Cora has information to share, as well as ideas of her own to contribute. And Tom, perhaps to play it safe, initially talks about the setting—a topic that is picked up on by others.

Clearly, early in the conversation, the individuals are reflecting on their own ideas, some thoughts are sparked by others, and they continue to build envisionments. Although they are not all coming from the same vantage point, nor building similar envisionments, a sense of openness and trust is pervasive. Joining in the conversation some time later, Rachel, who has been very quiet until now, feels ready to voice her concerns. Tom, too, eventually raises an essential issue that has been bothering him:

RACHEL: At the end, I was totally confused. I had to go back and see. I thought I had missed something with his name. How could he be, wait a minute, did I get his name mixed up. You know, but and I figured out she was gonna die. I thought it was horrible reading it. I was embarrassed. It was like things you never say out loud (*lots of laughter*) or read them in class. Embarrassing. I was embarrassed to read it. To think of people, you know, you may think it, but no.

DIANA: Well, you know, I kept thinking it was gonna turn into a fable, and that in fact Mrs. Mallard was a duck [Mrs. Mallard was the name of the main character]. Because, that was the extreme. Because, you know, sometimes fables are in the extreme about people, or about the characters are. But I had some of those things too.

TOM: As I was reading it, my first thing was trying to place it. Trying to fit it into something in my background that I could say, "Oh, this is a story, this genre, and this particular vein of a particular school," and then as I was reading, I was reflecting on my own particular grief that hearing a close friend had died some years ago. And then thinking of her reaction, similar to my parents' reaction and then when she got into the room, and the "Free, free, free." I was thinking Geez Martin Luther King, what's going on here? My mind jumped to pictures of Renoir or Van Gogh, pictures of France, and just the trying to open the windows, listening to the, it was almost a romantic setting of that picture in my mind. And then when I began to catch on that she was, and when I began to catch on to this feeling of liberation, freedom, that if you look back to D. H. Lawrence's *Lady Chatterley's Lover*, that whole literature, that whole feeling, that was there. That was kind of some of the things that were going through my mind. . . .

Because I had a guilty question. I wonder if my wife would feel that way if I suddenly died. And I guess I quickly dismissed it, no. (*Laughter*)

CORA: What about reversing it? What would men, do you think feel, if the wife died, and . . .

JANE: A sense of relief.

CORA: I'm sure you would.

TOM: I don't know, I just . . .

JUDITH: But it didn't occur to you when you were reading it though? You kept the same gender, you didn't . . .

TOM: Yeah, I didn't reverse it.

Here, both Rachel and Tom bring up issues that are of real concern to them that the others had not considered. Rachel's comment may have freed Tom to reveal his concern, since she was the first woman to voice discomfort with the piece. Although the others do not necessarily share either Rachel's or Tom's perspectives, they try to link their own experiences with those being voiced, consider their colleagues' perspectives, and explore related possibilities. Cora connects her own imaginings to Rachel's comments, and some of the women try to be supportive of Tom, yet guide him to consider the piece from a woman's (his wife's) perspective. They also consider Mr. Mallard's point of view. Still later in the conversation, they consider whether Mrs. Mallard's feelings of freedom are partly a psychological coping mechanism to get her through the initial sense of pain and mourning.

BARBARA: It's a possible interpretation, but looking at the piece of literature, I don't think the ending could be the same if *that* were the interpretation. If she's really denying the pain, then I don't think the ending fits the

JANE: I was gonna argue the other way. That if in fact her guilt was so great, if in fact it was a momentary thing, I mean I don't know that we know that she's been thinking these thoughts for a long time.

BARBARA: I think somewhere it's just that they never occurred to her.

DIANA: Paragraph 3 doesn't fit with denial. There's no denial there, there's immediate hearing and grieving.

Diana and Jane then read a couple of lines from the text, and the group continues exploring issues surrounding Mrs. Mallard's possible feelings of grief and joy (either or both). Based on her personal experience, Jane seems willing to consider the notion that Mrs. Mallard is in denial, but most of the others abandon it as unlikely. Still later, they focus on Kate

Chopin's life and the difficulties she faced writing in the Victorian era. They then discuss how these might have affected "Story of an Hour":

BARBARA: But you know, it almost, the story is almost made acceptable [for that era] by the way she dies at the end. It, had he not come back . . .
CORA: And [she] had a ball for the next 30 years
BARBARA: That's the part I think she couldn't write.

This was the group's first discussion. After getting to know one another better, the openness, willingness to assume others' perspectives, and willingness to disagree and confront one another increased greatly, but always with sensitivity and support. These are the types of discussions that students should learn to engage in, where they have room to explore topics that touch their lives, to use the text, related literature, and the author's life, as well as one another's and their own. What a preparation for life, if students can learn to interact in a community where their ideas can stimulate new awarenesses and possibilities, and where the reading of literature can assume a profound role in their human as well as cognitive development.

If you, as reader, take another look at the discussion of "Story of an Hour," you will see that there was some point-of-reference thinking (e.g., focused on the setting and on the problems Kate Chopin might have faced as an author). But primarily the group explored possibilities, building envisionments where overall understandings were left open and where there was always the potential to consider other issues.

The notion of valuing discussion—real conversation in which people interact with and build from one another's ideas—is not new. It was the basis of Dewey's (1899) call for experience-based education and of later generations of student-centered work (see, e.g., Barnes, 1976; Cazden, 1988; Mayher, 1990; Willinsky, 1991). My particular argument is that a shift in control from teacher to student is a necessary first step for the social interactions to shift from recitation and guesswork (What is it the teacher wants?) to substantive thought and discussion that can extend students' range of understanding.

TWO CLASSROOM EXPERIENCES

Let us look at Tanya Weber's first-grade class to see how such notions can possibly have relevance to 6-year-olds. Later, I compare this with a discussion in Maura Smythe's class of seniors who are a month away from high school graduation.

A First-Grade Reading Community

Tanya's classroom feels like a reading community. It is full of books. Bigger ones are stacked in bookcases in front of the windows; small ones are in baskets. More books stand open on tables. The baskets are scattered on the floor, some next to a "cushion corner," others near a colorfully pillowed couch. The couch has been turned into a cozy spot by adding a "roof," a yellow paper canopy stretched across four poles. This is one of the students' favorite reading places. The bulletin board is often dedicated to a "Star Author": Today, for instance, Jane Yolen's books are displayed. The classroom also has many "centers" for painting, science, math, and so forth. Next to the couch is a box containing cloth and other scraps that the children use to create costumes and scenes for their plays. The "story" area is bordered by the canopy couch on one side and a yellow armchair on the other. Between them is a green paper tree. Tanya often sits by the tree, reading aloud to her class.

The following discussion of *Sky Dogs* by Jane Yolen (1990) takes place in mid-November. It is part of a unit Tanya has developed "to do some consciousness-raising with my 6-year-olds about Native Americans." Three other books, a museum trip, photographs, and a local ethnography project examining cultural heritage will follow. Tanya sits under the tree as she reads *Sky Dogs*, a legend of how the Blackfeet first got horses. After discussing the author, Tanya guides the students' attention to the book.

Ms. WEBER: But, anyway, I'd like you to look at this beautiful, beautiful sky.

EMIL: It's a horse and an Indian. And it looks at . . .

SARA: The Native American.

Ms. WEBER: Well, Barry Moser is the illustrator.

BENJAMIN: He made a Native American wear a hat [the illustration depicts a fur hat and feather].

Ms. WEBER: Yes, it does.

EMIL: There is only one feather.

Ms. WEBER: Yes, that's right.

In this brief interaction, Tanya has invited the students to gather round and prepare to hear the story. They have already begun to anticipate what it will be about. Tanya begins. She is a wonderful storyteller and reads with a sense of warmth, emotion, and drama. Her voice invites the students into the piece.

Sky Dogs. By Jane Yolen. Illustrated by Barry Moser. My children, you asked me how did I come to be called "He Who Loves The Horses." For

now I sit in the tipi, and food is brought to me, and I do not ride the wind.
Come close—there, there. Come close, and I will tell you. Once the land
winded us, for we had to walk on our own legs from camp to camp, from
sky to sky, with only small dogs to carry our rawhide bags and pull the
travois sleds. The grass beneath our feet sang swee-swash, swee-swash,
and we wore out many moccasins along the paths of the plains. Then one
day we saw strange beasts, coming west of the mountains, coming from
Old Man's sleeping room.

JEFF: Where's the dogs?
JAMES: I can see them in the sky.
SARA: Now I can see them in the sky.
BENJAMIN: It looks like one of the footprints.
JAMES: This looks like one of his foots.
MS. WEBER: Oh! Hmmm.
JAMES: That looks like a foot.

The students have already begun participating in the storytelling event.
They use the illustrations, the story Tanya has already read, and one
another's comments to begin building envisionments. And they engage
in conversation. They listen to and share ideas with one another. Tanya
continues the reading.

They were so far away, we first thought they were long shadows. But the
sun was high, and still they came toward us, and that is not how a
shadow acts. Then we saw they were as big as an elk, with tails of straw.
Two Kutani clung to their backs, feet hanging down, like men who have
the sickness. And one beast pulled a heavily laden travois, like a big dog.
Then we were afraid. Jumps-Over-the-Water, who was my best friend and
was born in the same season, hid behind his mother's skirt. And Running
Bear, the bravest of us then, born a season sooner, ran behind the nearest
tipi. I stood apart and watched with big eyes, not because I was not afraid,
but because I could not move, because I had been caught out beyond the
safety of my father's tipi, beyond the safety of his arms. Often it was so
with me since my mother died. The men of our tribe made the mutterings
men make when they want to say, "We are not afraid. No. Not us. We are
mighty Piegan. We are warriors of the plains. We drove out the Kutani
and took their lands. We rule the wide grass from sky to sky." But they
were afraid. Their eyes grew big, and four of them reached out for their
hunting bows. That is because one may fear what comes from Old Man.

JEFF: Why are there horses instead of dogs?

JAMES: Maybe the mother like [unclear] but his father didn't like dogs.
Ms. WEBER: Hmm. That sounds like a good question. Can we think of that question while we're listening to the story?
MATT: That's the way the author, maybe he thinks it's a big dog that looks like a horse.
JAMES: No, but, it has a longer, it's bigger than a dog and dogs don't have faces like that?
Ms. WEBER: Does anyone else have a thought right now? Jeff is just so curious why these look like horses instead of dogs.
(A few students talk simultaneously)
BENJAMIN: We're brainstorming.

The students perceive a discrepancy between the grandfather's discussion of the animals he and his people thought were dogs, his descriptions of the animals, and the illustrations, and they begin working together to explore possibilities. Although she wants to get back to the story, Tanya realizes that the students need to work things through for themselves and supports them in doing so. For some time, the students use what they understand from the illustrations and the portion of the story they have just heard to discuss the issue. They consider whether the animals are real or imagined, whether both dogs and horses are interspersed in the field, and how the little boy and his tribespeople feel.

As the story continues, the children hear that three critically sick Kutani, two men and a woman, arrive. They are taken in and cared for by the boy's tribe, but the men soon die. While the elders care for the woman, the children play with the strange animals by throwing sticks for the animals to fetch. This does not work, and one of the animals runs away.

JAMES: Maybe because it wasn't a dog; it was a horse.
BENJAMIN: I know, maybe it was afraid and, horses think probably they are trying to kill it.
Ms. WEBER: Well, it sounds like you are much more sure now that we are definitely talking about horses.
JEFF: That was. Right when he said it, I was gonna say it. He said it though.
Ms. WEBER: What were you going to say, Jeff?

The children's discussion continues in much the same manner as the story unfolds. In this, as in all Tanya's literature reading groups, the students participate in a literary community that involves not only their active participation but interaction as well. They really interact, as did the readers we observed in the adult reading community; people talk to one another, listen to one another, and are responsive to one another's comments.

But this did not "just happen." Tanya believes that her students have come to school with many "story understanding" experiences and abilities they have learned as members of their other communities. It is this knowledge she wishes to tap and build upon, rather than ignore. She also believes that the students have important ideas of their own from which to weave understandings. To tap these abilities and ideas, and to invite the students into the ways of her literature group, she models what she calls "comments and reactions" by reading a piece and interspersing her reactions, demonstrating as well as telling the children that "there are no right or wrong ideas," only thoughts. Throughout the year, Tanya validates students' responses, always leaving room for reconsideration and further exploration. In the preceding example, the students learned to take charge of their own envisionment building, relying on the text, their own knowledge and experience, their classmates, and their teacher to move their thinking along. Even before being able to read from the text, they are fast becoming literate thinkers and active participants in literary discussions.

A Conversation Among Seniors

Now, let us look at Maura Smythe's class. She teaches in a comprehensive high school, grades 9–12, serving a largely college-oriented student body. Although the community is populated primarily by middle-class professional families, low-rent apartment complexes and two small rural working-class towns also lie within the school district. The course is a senior elective called Men, Women, and Literature. Maura created the course and has taught it for about 17 years. Her goal is to help students read, write, and think about complex gender issues. In the past, she started the course with readings on theoretical issues of gender, but this year, her focus is more literary. She says:

> Literary thinking involves putting yourself in the place of a character, and it involves an emotional level that sometimes doesn't get expressed intellectually [logically] but that affects readers in ways they are not conscious of. . . . I think of this as a much better way to approach the issue than a course in the feminist movement or a course in sociology that would have a unit on women and men. And I do think they get that idea. It's a better way because it's complex and allows for ambiguity . . . the kind of thinking you have to undergo.

Maura chose some thought-provoking pieces for this course, including some new pieces she had just read herself. Her classroom is large and is divided into an open area where her classes meet and a narrow area where computer and newspaper staff materials are located. (Maura is a faculty advisor for the school newspaper.) The students' desks are arranged in a circle. Two large tables are placed in the center of the circle and are used as a conference or work area, as needed. The bulletin boards contain a rich variety of materials, including newspaper articles and photographs that relate to Maura's courses. The students in Maura's class receive constant encouragement and affirmation, and Maura delivers her support with many smiles and personal expressions of her own pleasure in the activity. Of the 25 students in this course, 6 are male and 19 are female.

At this point in the year, the students have already read *The Bean Trees* by Barbara Kingsolver (1989) and *Sula* by Toni Morrison (1974). They are now reading a series of short stories. The following discussion, in response to "The Abortion" by Alice Walker (1990), is representative of the others. This story is about a well-educated African American couple who live in the South. The husband is a legal advisor to the mayor, with political ambitions of his own. The wife remains home alone much of the time, caring for their 2-year-old daughter. He is preoccupied with his work, distant in their relationship, and the marriage is suffering. She has recently learned that she is pregnant but does not want another child. He is absorbed by the pressures of his work, and she is left to face an abortion alone and, eventually, to end the marriage. Maura begins the discussion as she usually does:

Ms. SMYTHE: All right, who'd like to start?

SIKKA: Well I didn't like her at all. I thought that she had the right to have the abortion, and she felt that she needed this. And she said something. She said she chose herself over the child. She wasn't even thinking about what she was doing.

Ms. SMYTHE: Did she think about it before that, or . . .

SIKKA: I mean, she had thought about it, but she was completely selfish about it. She never, I don't think she looked at what was really happening.

RAINA: I totally disagree. I liked it. I mean, there were parts in it that upset me a lot. Abortion is not really my belief, and she had two abortions, but that's like not for me to judge. But generally, I liked the way she personalized the whole thing. She just let you know the situation. And she led you through.

Ms. SMYTHE: Did you think she was selfish?

RAINA: I can't, in my opinion, I think she was selfish. She had to choose. Like I've been in situations where you have to choose yourself or somebody else, and the only thing you can do is choose yourself. She like put it that way.

CAROL: I agree with Sikka, because she was just totally, like she wrote she can't imagine another child, even to her husband. He like brought her tea, and she said, "I can't drink that. Take it away." She's just being mean about the whole thing.

CLAUDIA: [unclear] Maybe like what she says isn't exactly how she feels, she can't really pinpoint it. Sometimes when people are in that kind of situation, what they say isn't what they mean. Like when you're angry at someone and you don't mean what you say.

Thus far, a number of the students have voiced their initial impressions, but they are hesitant, leaving themselves open for additional ideas. They listen to one another, picking up on earlier comments, and providing their own ideas. Claudia's comment seems to provide a new perspective for them to consider and move beyond. See the focus change:

HAIKA: I don't know. [unclear] It was okay when she refused the tea, but when she started making him sleep in the guest room.
(A few students talk simultaneously)
HAIKA: It went on a really long time.
RAINA: Yeah, but he was being a jerk. Wouldn't get the surgery [vasectomy] done.
BEV: I know. He shouldn't have to. That's like . . .
RAINA: I mean, like she's the one who's gonna be pregnant. He doesn't get pregnant, so it doesn't really affect him. It affects him, but not directly. I mean, it's not his body that's gonna get affected by it. Somebody had to get the surgery done.
HAIKA: Yeah, but there's other methods, and also she was really unstable about their marriage. Unless you're sure you're really going to be with that man, you shouldn't cut off his options.
CLAUDIA: But so, she should cut off hers?
HAIKA: Yeah, if that's what she wants.
HARRY: She's the one that didn't want the kid.

Here, the students raise critical issues of feelings, intentions, options, and actions. They begin to explore the issues from many perspectives, including those of the characters within the piece as well as the students within the class. For a while, they explore the characters' lives, the era, and related occurrences in the story. They seem to be trying to get to know the characters and their situation better as a way to further develop their own understandings of the piece. Later, Harry's comment shifts the focus again:

HARRY: I don't know, I really didn't like the lady at all, so, the whole story is told from her perspective.

CLAUDIA: Yeah, well, I mean he didn't really go with her. Sitting there talking about political discussion on the way to the airport. He dumped her off. It was her business, her life, so she takes care of it. He wasn't very supportive.

SAM: But also, she's a pain about it. Like, you know, I don't care if you try to be nice, get the tea away from me. And what was it, go sleep in the guest room.

CLAUDIA: That was after, that wasn't like before. Maybe she was just mad that . . .

MS. SMYTHE: Describe their relationship. All these stories [the short stories they are reading] are about relationships. What kind of marriage is this?

Although Claudia begins to discuss the husband's behavior, Jen and Claudia then recycle ideas already discussed. Maura suggests a topic to help them continue their exploration. After a time, they tackle more complex issues while continuing to serve as both sounding boards and springboards for other ideas.

RICK: But I think there was a place, that she would never, like she thought she'd never get a husband that was this caring, or something like that. If there was someone that would leave, it would be her. So, like, I think she was mad about a lot of things but she never really left what she did. And it was just a weird relationship 'cause she knew that she was in control. He knew that he could never leave her.

MS. SMYTHE: Is he portrayed as good?

RICK: Yeah, I think she's maybe, I don't think he's a bad guy or anything, but I think he should have taken a little more time with her and not just dropped her off. Should have been in their discussions. But, I think she kind of jumped the gun a couple of times on him. He says something like, "We'll talk about it later," and she gets all mad.

MS. SMYTHE: Other reactions to their relationship?

PAULA: 'Cause this is important to her, and his attention to politics. She saw him just blowing it off. I think it showed that they had nothing in common. I think that's when she realized she's leaving.

As the discussion continues, the students also consider the husband's preoccupation with his job, and whether it was in fact the husband's way of providing, in Harry's words, "advancement for the whole family." The issues of control and essential unhappiness are discussed again and how they relate to the characters and their interactions. As is usual in Maura's classes, the discussion ends with many students still exploring their questions, still in the process of developing their own envisionments of the piece. Sometimes Maura brings critical analyses to class for her students to read, but only after they have completed discussions of this sort, where they have had an opportunity to develop understandings and consider issues on their own.

THE CREATION OF COMMUNITIES

Although "The Abortion" and the issues it raises are far more mature than those considered by Tanya's first-grade class, we can see many similarities in the ways in which the two classes function. They are both interactive and supportive communities where students feel comfortable speaking their minds, and no one is shut out. Even though there are some basic disagreements in Maura's class about the issues of abortion and gender roles, the students engage in dialogue with one another. Diverse opinions echo in the discussion in a way that adds complexity and sensitivity to students' understandings of the characters and their situations.

Discussions of this sort are new to both of these teachers and their classes. Tanya explained the changes she was making:

I see that I need to provide situations where I will "sit out" and really build the community so that the children can talk to each other, enhancing their ideas. I want to be quiet more and an active listener more . . . I didn't understand at all [before] about helping students take another perspective.

Maura's comments are similar:

I've really changed since I've [started to focus on envisionment building] in that my approach, I would never ever have asked something about how you felt right at the end [referring to her opening question after a reading]. I would usually ask what questions came up, and then we would usually look at specific parts and I sometimes did that because it allowed everyone to participate even if they hadn't done the assignment. But it was very frustrating because it didn't really teach them how to figure out what parts were important for themselves. . . . Now I have become more conscious of teachers' decisions in general. I am starting to see the distinctions among the stances as I hear students speaking from different positions. . . . I see how the group works to help each other's thinking.

In literary communities of the sort Tanya and Maura are developing, there is room for individual students to form their own responses. Students in their classes, however, do not operate apart from the group. During discussion and all other activities in the class, the students hear and consider others' ideas and comments; they expect that those views will interest them and will move their own thinking along. Here, students begin by thinking about their own envisionments at the end of a selection, but they soon go beyond. The first comment shared by a classmate has the potential to set a student thinking, exploring, and moving beyond the envisionment that she or he had a moment before.

From this perspective, a student's response is not a "personal response," in the sense of being limited to an individual's personal thoughts alone. Too often, notions of student response are trivialized, used in a limited fashion to refer only to thoughts about the student's life that connect with the work being read. I think it is more useful to think of response as coming from the envisionments students have at any point in time, which will change based on further thinking and discussion with others. When students are responding, their interpretations are in the process of forming and changing. Response and interpretation are not sequential, interpretation following response, but co-occur within the complex web of envisionment building.

Students use their interactions with others to explore new horizons of possibilities. Such explorations help students see from various angles of vision, providing them with increasing sensitivity to the complexities in life as well as in literature. And from this comes their growing ability to understand the options people seem to have before them in literature and life—as well as the ability to explore and find new ones.

Through such interactions, students learn to develop their own capabilities as thinkers and participants in the complex social relations of the class and the broader community. As they learn to listen to and confront one another, students enter into dialogue in the sense that Bakhtin (1981) describes. Such dialogue permits participants to consider other ways of interpreting and to view the individual selves within the class community as interwoven; the participants, and thus the community itself, are open to difference, empathy, awareness, and change. In this environment, students learn to treat literature in ways that enrich their personal development, critical thought, thinking abilities, and understandings of social differences and connectedness. These are qualities that they will continue to use as literate and humane thinkers throughout their lives.

5

A Practical Pedagogy

Across much of modern educational history, school reform in English language arts has focused primarily on ways to teach—on what lessons should look like and how they should proceed. Underlying such reform was the belief that something was wrong and needed to be fixed, and that changes in what teachers did would fix it. Reforms have focused on such issues as group size (e.g., whole class, small group, individualized), materials (e.g., anthologies and basal readers, prepackaged literature collections, abridged texts, "great" books, library or trade books, multicultural texts, cultural units), mode of interaction (e.g., lecture, discussion, peer groups, computer), mode of instruction (e.g., direct instruction, guided instruction, student inquiry), and conceptions of language and literature learning (e.g., whole language, constructivist, reader response, new critical).

These reform movements were generally accompanied by particular teaching methods that teachers were expected to learn. In a desire to ensure equal education, all teachers were expected to be doing the same thing, and so were their students. There was a preferred kind of teaching and learning being sought, and a preferred way to do it.

Although these reforms were meant to make substantive changes in what students learned, they were what Cuban (1984) described as waves atop an otherwise still ocean; students did different things in class, but what the students thought about and learned did not essentially change. He suggests that reforms have been ineffective because they have not changed underlying beliefs about the kind of learning and knowing that counts in schools. As long as the mark of bright, successful learners remains the acquisition of facts and skills, the replication and recitation of plot summaries, titles, and authors' meanings, that is what students will focus on and learn, despite changes in instructional approach (J. A. Langer, 1984).

This should come as no surprise. The social view of learning I described earlier makes clear that students learn what a community values. Students learn what they are taught, they learn to do it better, and they are rewarded for such learning by the people and system around them.

I am describing an essential tension in education: The ways in which we want students to think and learn are not necessarily connected to underlying beliefs held either by the field or by the public about what counts as thinking and knowing. On the one hand, we cling to old conceptions of learning; on the other, we want essential changes to take place. Historically, we have misattributed "failure" because we did not attend to an essential ingredient, the practical day-to-day workings of classrooms, including participants' beliefs about what it meant to do "well."

Let us approach this issue by considering how the notion of envisioning literature can best work for teachers and their students. From my perspective, one essential given is that all envisionment-building classrooms do not necessarily have to look the same way, nor do the teachers or their students have to behave in the same way (Langer & Applebee 1987). There are, however, a set of theoretical beliefs about what counts as learning and knowing that need to be at the center of teachers' goals and of students' understandings about the focus of their learning. These include the concepts introduced in earlier chapters: the importance of envisionment building and exploration of possibilities; the need for students to learn to control and develop their own inquiry and move toward fuller understandings; and the use of literature for social, personal, critical, and cognitive development.

PRINCIPLES OF PRACTICE

We have already seen accounts of classrooms in action, such as Maura's and Tanya's. Both teachers were working to create lively literary communities in their classrooms, and reading about their experiences has undoubtedly stirred a variety of ideas in the readers of this book. With all the differences among classes, there are similar pedagogical principles that apply when students are engaged in exploring horizons of possibilities, building envisionments, pursuing their inquiries of literature and life. First I discuss these principles and then illustrate how they work during a week in Barbara Furst's seventh-grade class.

At an essential level, the overriding ethos of the thoughtful "envisioning literature" classroom is the belief that literature *is* thought provoking and that students *are* competent thinkers. I cannot stress this enough:

These two beliefs permeate and "mark" the culture of the envisionment-building classroom. When these are present, students and teachers assume that when they pick up a literary work they will enter what Benton (1992) calls a "secondary world," where minds explore horizons of possibilities and imaginations soar. This is the nature of the literary experience, expected as a naturally occurring experience in an envisionment-building literature class.

This might seem like a fairly common attribute of many classrooms, but unfortunately, it is not. In classes where the goal is surface understandings and received interpretations, literature is not treated as thought provoking but as answer giving (J. A. Langer, 1992). For this type of class to become centrally concerned with what students think about and how they think, the community must develop a real and consistent understanding that literature *is* thought provoking and that the way to engage in the literary experience is to *be* thoughtful. Such are the beliefs that underlie the four principles that follow. They pervade the envisionment-building literature classroom.

1. *Students are treated as lifelong envisionment builders.* We have seen in earlier chapters that students have spent their lives building envisionments in their efforts to make sense of themselves and their worlds. Effective teaching and learning begin with the recognition that students in class use this knowledge, acquired during a lifetime, to create their own text-worlds (or envisionments) during their experiences with literature. They use their past experiences with literature, literacy, and life as threads from which to weave new understandings, new takes on their reading of each piece. Teachers recognize that each and every student *can* and *does* make sense of every literary experience. Each individual does so with the stories told or heard in everyday life and can, therefore, do so in school.

Teaching and learning environments that regard students as lifelong envisionment builders legitimate students as thinkers in their classrooms and unhesitatingly invite them to further develop their understandings. In classroom cultures of this sort, students take ownership for their own developing ideas; they use the knowledge they came to school with to make sense, observe others, and seek assistance when they think they need it. From this perspective, teaching involves becoming a careful listener (a kid-watcher, as Yetta Goodman [1985] calls it), trying to understand students' ideas and helping them find ways to work through the ideas that must be worked through in every act of envisionment building.

Tanya's and Maura's classes offer clear examples of classroom cultures where the exploration of literature involves students as envisionment builders, thinking for themselves and communicating with one another as they look forward to possibilities they have not yet explored. Here, students are treated as individuals who are thinkers, who necessarily have ownership for their own ideas, and who exist in a community of other cothinkers and friends. As I discussed in Chapter 4, in social settings of this sort, students behave thoughtfully because the classroom culture calls for it. Instead of leading them to thoughts that are not their own, the interactions provide students with the space to pursue their own ideas and thus to become more adept envisionment builders, more powerful thinkers, and more thoughtful human beings.

2. *Questions are treated as part of the literary experience.* The very act of sense making in literature is open-ended and inquisitive, in search of new horizons. Thus, in an essential way, the literary experience *involves* the raising of questions; questions are necessary and normal when a person is exploring horizons of possibilities. This is why every envisionment is filled with questions and hunches as well as more fully developed ideas, even after much thought and discussion have taken place. From the perspective of envisionment building, we would expect a person to have all sorts of questions about her or his understandings at the moment, about what might develop, about connections to other literature, about relationships to life. "I'm not sure . . . " "What if . . . ?" "Did you really think that . . . ?" People ask such questions when making sense of literature outside of school—after seeing a movie, when discussing a best-seller, and during the intermission of a play. Such questions indicate that the person is actively building envisionments—*is* a literary thinker. In the examples we have already examined, the role of such questions is just as clear among adults discussing "The Story of an Hour" as it is among the students whose classes we have examined.

When we view questions as a central way in which understandings develop, instruction becomes a time to help students explore possibilities, not merely to resolve uncertainties but to move beyond: considering alternatives, weighing evidence, and developing yet other questions. Tanya Weber and Barbara Furst, for example, help their students learn to become good questioners and to use their questions as a way to deepen their understandings. They ask their students (working in groups or alone) to come up with questions that will be interesting to discuss in class and to raise questions during class time that will help extend the group's perspectives and invite them to explore possibilities.

In text-based classrooms, having a question can carry a negative connotation; it can signify that a student "doesn't know" something, was not a "good" reader. It is no surprise that students in such classroom communities often do not like to ask questions. However, in classrooms that support envisionment building, the asking of questions is considered a desirable behavior, indicating that students who consider uncertainties and explore possibilities are being *good* readers of literature.

3. *Class meetings are a time to develop understandings.* Because the notion of developing envisionments treats understandings as fluid and changing, the very purpose of class meetings becomes to help participants explore and further develop their understandings. The teacher and the students take for granted that their thoughts about the piece as they enter the class will change before they leave, and that the class meeting is an opportunity to explore and move beyond those earlier ideas. In this context, students (and also their teachers) explore the uncertainties and hunches they bring with them and consider other possibilities and perspectives as a result of interacting as part of the group.

From the perspective of envisionment building, discussion begins with students' initial impressions, the ideas they have at a particular point in time, which are expected to change. Students often convey ideas from within their envisionments as questions or hunches—provisional comments that lead the group into a fuller range of explorations. In this way, class meetings are times when students individually and collectively participate in reworking their interpretations, raising questions, exploring possibilities, and getting deeper into the piece as collaborative group members, each from his or her perspective as an individual.

4. *Multiple perspectives are used to enrich interpretation.* In envisionment-building classrooms, multiple perspectives are of great importance. Considering others' perspectives works in a number of ways: as a way to help students reflect on ideas that did not initially come to mind, as a way to confront their own ideas more reflectively (and more analytically) in comparison to or in conflict with others, as a way to develop interpretations based on particular points of view, and as a way to gain sensitivity in response to perspectives that are not their own. Multiple perspectives not only help students develop and analyze their own understandings, they also add patina—layers of complexity that enrich the envisionments students create and the ways in which they see themselves, their lives, and the world.

Across the grades, teachers can help their students take perspectives in a variety of ways from both within and outside the selection. Students can discuss the piece from their own perspectives as well as from the perspectives of the individual characters. (We saw Maura's students doing this as they pondered the situation in "The Abortion" from their own, the husband's, and the wife's perspectives.) They can also consider the piece from the perspective of other works they have read and experienced, as well as other cultures and traditions. Through perspective taking, students gain breadth of understanding within their own envisionments, and with it an increased understanding of the subjectivity and contextuality of meaning and thus a better understanding of other people's perspectives.

For the most part, students explore horizons of possibilities when they take perspectives, treating the issues they raise subjectively and in an open-ended manner. However, at times, they need to objectify the character or experience—holding a certain characterization steady for a moment in time in order to inspect it from a particular vantage point. Such explorations permit students to engage in the kind of point-of-reference thinking they take up when acting as literary and critical theorists. In such explorations, they may bring one or another set of "external" criteria or frames of reference to bear upon the work, examining it from, for example, a feminist or Freudian perspective, or judging its structural coherence.

This treatment of perspective taking assumes that there is no one "best" interpretation. Rather, interpretation is in the eyes of the beholder. An individual's transaction with the text and the envisionments that develop are inextricably related to that individual's personal, cultural, historical, social, and academic experiences. Perspective taking is a way to develop, challenge, and round out one's own views and to understand where differences in interpretation emanate.

Together, these four principles underlie a classroom culture where the literary environment *exemplifies* as well as *considers* issues of ethics, civic and social responsibility, cultural identity, aesthetics, and reasoning—as they relate to literature, self, and others.

A CLASS IN ACTION

To see what these principles look like in practice, let us look at one of Barbara Furst's seventh-grade classes as the students engage in a weeklong project involving "All Summer in a Day" by Ray Bradbury (1954/1992). This is a short story about a brief time in the lives of a class of 9-year-olds who live on the planet Venus, where it rains almost all the time, except for an hour every 7 years, when the sun comes out. Margot, who was born on Earth (and may soon return), is the only child in her class who remembers what the look and warmth of the sun are like. The other children are jealous. The teacher leaves the room for a moment just before the scheduled appearance of the sun, and William (the class ringleader) and Margot's other classmates lock her in the closet.

When the teacher returns, she takes the students outdoors to greet the sun, all except Margot. The children play happily in the sun until the rain begins anew. When the children return to their underground class-room, they remember Margot and silently unlock the door to let her out.

Barbara teaches this story almost every year; she says, "It's very accessible for middle graders. Very real for the kids." As is her pattern with all readings, she teaches it differently each year, depending on the students in her class and the kinds of interactions with literature she feels are appropriate. "Their needs are different. One year I taught it early in the year for social reasons. The kids were doing pretty cruel things and [I] wanted them to have a chance to talk things out." Later Barbara added, "I think the language Bradbury uses is very interesting and would like to spend more time on it, but I always try to figure out where the kids need to go." In the last year or two, Barbara has shown them a movie based on the story after they have read and discussed it. The movie depicts a happy ending, which previous classes seemed to like. However, they did not compare the movie ending with their own sadder envisionments; instead, they seemed to "buy into" the movie's depic-tion. Barbara felt that the students in this class also tended to defer to "sanctioned" interpretations, including movie depictions, without the questioning and reflection they had come to expect when engaging with one another's interpretations.

To help her students learn to question the movie as well as one an-other, Barbara planned a series of activities to focus on imagery, both as they envisioned it and as the movie depicted it. Following the usual pattern in this class, throughout this activity, the students did a lot of freewriting, using their notes as a basis for various kinds of small group discussions. They participated in small group discussions almost daily, during which they extended their own ideas and selected key issues for the whole class to think about and discuss. Because they used their present envisionments as a way to begin rethinking, everyone expected their ideas to change. Thus discussion was exploratory. Literary discus-sions are an important source of new ideas and a forum for thinking through the ones students are forming.

Intrinsic to all Barbara's interactions with her students is a focus on their developing envisionments. She lets them know in many ways that the only wrong answer is no answer; *their* ideas are the focus of the class meetings—without them, there would be a void.

Barbara's class is a heterogeneous and mainstreamed group. It con-tains a wide range of students with different social, academic, and physi-cal histories. For example, Nicole and Rebecca are both profoundly deaf. A certified interpreter who uses sign language serves as an intermediary, signing to the students and translating their signs to oral speech. In this way, both girls are actively involved in all class activities, including the discussion that follows.

Day One

On the first day of the "All Summer in a Day" project, Barbara and her students discuss reading the story in a way that would enable them to plan how to present it as a movie. They talk about imagery and its role in conveying one's understanding. Then Barbara begins reading the story aloud, engaging the students as envisionment builders from the outset. She asks her students to make a movie of the story in their minds, letting the scenes develop and change as the story and their thoughts move on. She stops twice along the way and again at the end for the students to jot down what they are thinking. "What do you think is happening? What do you see?" Her goal here and throughout the entire unit is to help her students become more aware of their envisionments, thus making their ideas, questions, and hunches available for them to talk and think about.

Throughout the year, Barbara occasionally reads to her class to dramatize a piece that she thinks they might be less familiar with, and the students often do a similar envisionment-building activity by jotting the ideas and questions they are thinking about along the way. This time, however, they are focusing more on scenes. The quickwrites of two students at three different points in the story help us see the students' growing impressions of the piece. The spelling and punctuation appear as they do in the students' own journals.

Manny writes:

Well, first I see the planet. I see any streets flooded. All the forests are like marshland and there are many insects flying everywhere. The sky is always cloudy and the plants look small and sickly.

Later, he writes:

I think missing the sight of the sun may drive Margo a bit crazy. She seems to be almost there anyway, protesting to let water touch her hand. I picture William as the popular kid everyone laughing at whatever pitiful jokes he makes. The whole class is jealous of Margo's escape. There quite cruel.

And at the end:

What an ending. Margo missed the only sunlight in 7 years. How will she act? Will she hate the kids? Will they apologize? I thought Margo would have a chance to see it. At least it had a realistic ending.

Anne-Marie writes:

I see a group of children mushed all together at several large windows. The windows are covered in little droplets of water. The children are small and anxious and pushing and shoving to get to the front.

Later on in her reading, she writes:

I can see the little children watching the window. The sound of hard hitting rain is still falling. Then all of a sudden there is silence. A peaceful bliss of silence. I was also surprised by the children's behavior. Locking someone in the closet is not civilized behavior.

And at the end:

This story ended very abruptly and didn't really wrap itself up. But I do think I know why though. The whole story centered around Margo. The children took her only chance (probably) to see the sun and not have to live in a rainfilled world.

In these quickwrites, it is clear that both Manny's and Anne-Marie's envisionments change over time. Although they have not had time to reflect on the story, we see them grappling with their first brief meeting with the piece. They are formulating initial ideas, raising questions, and developing some critical reactions to the work. These in-process jottings help the students focus on their envisionments, inviting them to inspect their own text-worlds, anticipate where their ideas might take them, and become aware of their changing envisionments.

Barbara's students frequently do such quickwrites in response to what they are reading, thinking, or discussing. It is a way for them to reflect on their own thoughts for and by themselves; the quickwrites help them draw on relevant knowledge and experiences, consolidate and review ideas, and reformulate and extend their understandings. In this case, the quickwrites help the students consolidate and review the ideas they have begun to create.

For homework, Barbara asks the students to read the story on their own and to come to class the next day with "some questions you think we need to talk about." Barbara frequently gives her students this task as a homework assignment, treating questions as a natural part of the literary experience.

Here are some questions that Manny brings with him. We see that the characters' perspectives are already a concern.

> Well, first of all I think we should talk about Margot reaction when she's let out of the closet. We, as a class, may come up with a few ideas based on Margot's character. I think she may be more distant or cry horribly.
>
> Next I think we should discuss whether the fact that if it is scientifically wrong, should that matter. I don't believe so. It's a short story to make one think and enjoy, not to pick apart and analyze. It's science *FICTION* not meant to be realistic. . . .
>
> I'd also like to talk about William's role. An influential, popular person, or a bully everyone fears.

Anne-Marie writes:

> I think we need to talk more about Margot. Margot is very hard to understand. Her position in the story needs to be verified. And the childrens' behavior also needs to be looked at. It's all very confusing to me. . . .
>
> The setting is also giving me trouble. The author needs to put a little more effort into looking at the description of the school.
>
> The teacher is unclear too. Where is she? Is she the person who is having the conversation throughout the beginning of the piece?
>
> We also need to say that we can imagine the answers to all questions. Its a Science Fiction piece. We can believe anything we want.

Both Manny and Anne-Marie think they need to discuss Margot; she is the central character, yet subtly characterized. Manny wants to discuss William's behavior, and Anne-Marie wants to discuss the children's behavior. They realize that Margot and her classmates are important to talk about, central to gaining a deeper understanding of the story. Both students are also aware that aspects of the story are likely untrue and thus think that a discussion of the genre would help them better understand the piece. Although we have seen that Manny's and Anne-Marie's envisionments are not the same, both know that these are important issues if they are to understand the piece in greater depth. They also know that their class meetings are always the time to raise and explore questions such as these.

From experience, all the students in Barbara's class have come to expect that questions will be treated as concerns that are the result of and lead to understandings; class is considered a time to develop understandings, and multiple perspectives are explored as a way to enrich understanding. They intuitively accept the underlying principles as the way learning gets done in Barbara's class.

Day Two

In class the next day, the students form small groups, as they often do, to discuss their questions and formulate a few questions to pose to the entire class. As the groups form, Barbara makes the purpose overt: "We need to know what people are thinking about to get us started in the discussion, and I'm gonna go over to this group because they had so many questions; then, as we go along, we may see that some questions are actually part of a bigger issue we need to look at."

The students' interactions are lively, provocative, and exploratory. They raise questions, pose and explore possibilities, disagree and argue with one another. In some instances, the discussion moves students' envisionments along so rapidly that the questions they brought with them become irrelevant, and other new questions become more pertinent. In other cases, earlier questions remain important to explore and keep being raised. In all cases, the questions, useful as entry points, are treated as fluid; they are used only if needed to provoke relevant discussion in a context in which ideas are always changing.

Before leaving their group seating arrangement, the students in each group have not only discussed their concerns but are also prepared with questions for the whole class to consider. Barbara writes their questions on the board and helps the students link new questions with ones already suggested, clustering them into larger issues as she had mentioned earlier. Here, we see all four principles operating simultaneously. Because the students are treated as lifelong envisionment builders with ideas of their own, Barbara and the others accept all ideas. Question asking is frequently used to voice concerns and explore horizons of possibility. Because class is treated as a time to develop understandings, Barbara (and the other students) help particular students clarify the concerns they raise, legitimating the issues and making them more available to think about and discuss. And multiple perspectives are used as a normal way to enrich interpretations. The discussion begins with the issue of style and form.

BRAD: Why did the author put so many short sentences in all of the short paragraphs?

Ms. FURST: Are you talking about short sentences, or are you talking about the description?

BRAD: Yeah, why were there, like, such short paragraphs?

Ms. FURST: All right, so why so many short paragraphs? What are you really asking about? So, what are you asking about? All right, so you're asking, the issue here is how the author wrote the story. His style that he chose to write the story in. That's an important issue. One that you can look at in any story we read is, why did the author write it this way? Why did he choose to have so many short paragraphs? Didn't you also have a question, I'm just remembering, about description. What was the question about description?

BRAD: I think that's number (*reads number from his group's list*). Why did the author use some of the description?

Ms. FURST: Okay. Why descriptive words, or the paragraph. That's again another question about why did the author write this story this way. Now, what other questions do you have?

Barbara helps Brad clarify the questions his group raised, and the students go on to question why the people happened to be on Venus in the first place and why William instigated such an insidious prank.

ANNE-MARIE: Why were the people living in Venus for seven years when it was raining?

Ms. FURST: So, you're asking why did those people choose to live there? Are you talking about the choices they make? Okay. What else?

KEVIN: Why did the boy feel that he was a bully?

Ms. FURST: Can I just go with William's behavior? Why did he behave the way he did? So, the issue over here that we're looking at, this one here is a little different, one of a settler's motivation for being on Venus and the other you want to look at is William's behavior.

DIERDRE: So quiet, and she really kept to herself, and why were they picking on her?

Ms. FURST: Two questions—why Margo behaved that way and why the children. We're looking at Margo's behavior and the other children.

Here, Barbara helps the students clarify and relate their ideas but does not interpose her own. The question-asking activity serves as the beginning of the discussion, provoking ideas and helping the students consider issues they had not necessarily addressed, as fodder for envisionment building. The students then move into the discussion circle, a large circle of chairs that permits them to look at one another.

Ms. Furst: What we need to do is, you need to decide where we need to start. Do you want to focus on (*she reads their questions from the board*)? Where do you want to start? Do you want to go somewhere else?

Instead of beginning with the items on the board, the students bring up a couple of new issues. Because envisionments are always in a state of change, with new ideas constantly coming to mind, and because the purpose of the discussion is to develop understandings, it is irrelevant to Barbara whether the questions the students raise are on the board or not. If the ideas are in their envisionments, they are appropriate for discussion. Barbara knows that raising the questions and connecting the issues serve as a way for the students to develop ideas, bring other thoughts to mind, and develop new ideas to address. First, Manny asks about particular language used in the story, and other students join in. They think that figurative language might be provocative in understanding the characters.

Manny: Why did the author say the children look like so many leaves ["like leaves before a hurricane"] and so many roses?
Ms. Furst: Okay, so what was your sense of that?
Manny: I think they came from all over the world and settled on Venus.
Ms. Furst: Keep going.
Manny: When I hear leaves, it's bad and roses are good.
Mike: Yeah.
Ms. Furst: People want to respond to that one?
Rebecca: I think there were some good kids, and some bad kids, but all of this moment they were the same people. They were the same person looking out and waiting for the sun to come out. . . .
Dierdre: We need to go through those reasons, because I would consider Margo a rose, and she was like, and kids who locked her in the closet, I would think of them as leaves—trying to keep the rose away. And then, it can also be that they're all different, they came from all over the world.
Ms. Furst: Someone want to comment?

The students brainstorm their associations, and then the significance of roses and leaves is set aside as Kurt changes the topic to why the people stayed on Venus, with its inhospitable conditions.

KURT: I want to go to something different.

Ms. FURST: All right, go ahead. Where do you want to go Kurt?

KURT: I was a little curious why the people even stayed in Venus. I mean it's raining for seven years. They don't like it.

Ms. FURST: Why didn't they leave?

KURT: Yeah.

Ms. FURST: All right, so? (*Looks at the students, inviting them to speak*)

MANNY: I think they stayed there because they were like, it's an exploration. They're paying a lot of money to be there. If Margo's family comes back, they'll lose a lot of money. . . . I mean, you have to work, but you don't necessarily have to hate your job, or to get money just for like living there. Go up there and have it rain.

ROCK: Well, we probably don't know. We've just had weeks where it's been raining, and disgusting, and you feel horrible, I mean 'cause the sun isn't out and when the sun is out you get more energy, you get more pep. . . . They did something like that on "20/20" where they had, people would get into depressions because they needed the sun.

Ms. FURST: So, you're having the same kind of puzzlement that Kurt is having, you don't believe that we, our human race here, would survive very well in that environment? Rita Mae?

RITA MAE: All the children have been there for so long, and they can't imagine it with the sun, but once they did [unclear] what it would be like because it's something we're used to. And also, I have something else. Why would people, it's in the future. How do we know what Earth was? Earth could be so [unclear] and disgusting that nobody would even want to be there.

ANNE-MARIE: The other thing is what do you eat? There's nothing to eat. There's nothing to make the plants grow.

Ms. FURST: All right, really talking about how you're seeing the setting. Nicole, you wanted to say something?

NICOLE: I was gonna say the same thing.

Ms. FURST: About what, which part of it?

NICOLE: If something happened to Earth, you know, if it was polluted or something like that.

Ms. FURST: So there's a possibility these people may be up there because there's a better life than staying on Earth.

KURT: They didn't they were jealous that Margo was gonna go back
to Earth. And Margo will go back to Earth, so I don't see why
there, I don't think the pollution . . .

Then, they cycle back to questions of why the characters behaved as they
did, this time focusing on why the teacher had not noticed Margot's
absence.

MANNY: My other question is the teacher. Is this such a large class
that she missed Margo?
MS. FURST: So what about that? What are you trying to say?
MANNY: Why didn't the teacher miss her?

The discussion continues, with the students weaving back and forth
among questions of content, language, and form. Although most of
the talk centers on content (e.g., why the characters acted as they did,
why they lived on Venus), the students also focus on the language as
a source of meaning (e.g., metaphorical uses of roses and leaves). In
time, all the questions on the board are discussed, except for the author's
style (form). The board notes are not used as a reminder, but the students bring up these same issues in the context of their discussion (some
issues they cycle back to several times) because they still need to work
them through. The discussion is lively, with students continuing to talk
after class.

At home they do quickwrites, which they add to their folders and use
for the next group meeting. The quickwrites provide the students (and
Barbara) with a window on their envisionments at that point in time and
as they are poised to go forward toward new ideas. Throughout, the
quickwrites help the students not only draw on relevant knowledge and
experiences from their envisionments and general experiences but also
consolidate, review, reformulate, and extend their understandings
(Langer & Applebee, 1987). For example, Rock writes:

In the discussion, I think we need to hit on specifically the characters and behaviors and actions that go with them. The teacher and
Margo and William are all strong characters with majorly question-
able roles in this piece. Also, I think we should get into the ending.
This piece finishes abruptly and leaves you hanging (exactly the
authors plan) but It should be discussed what could happen next
and the feelings of the classroom.

Dierdre writes:

I think we still need to talk a little more about the teacher. I don't understand the significance of having her in the story. I think we also need to talk about the conditions of weather, how the scientists would know that the sun was going to come out that day.

We should also talk about why these families went to Venus in the first place, How many people were living on Venus, what did they eat. There is probably a lot more to talk about but thats all I can think of at the moment.

Rock and Dierdre, like the other students in Barbara's class, are behaving as lifelong envisionment builders, raising good questions that are meaningful to them, and taking responsibility for understanding the interplay of voices within the story as they develop their own thoughts.

Day Three

The next day, in small groups, the students discuss their questions and plan what they might include in their movie script of the story. While they discuss their ideas with others, they are reminded to remain true to their own understanding of the story and to refer to their folders for ideas. To help them focus on their own envisionments, each student fills in a brief sheet about the following: the characters and scenes they consider essential, any changes they would make, and the way they would end the movie.

During these movie-making discussions, the students delve more deeply into the characters, their motivations, and their behaviors. They also consider the situation from a variety of perspectives. In the following examples, we can see the students' differing interpretations taking shape, including how they as directors would structure the final scene.

Manny, who sees the hurtfulness of gossip and imagines a relenting William, writes:

> Instead of using flashbacks, I'd focus on small conversations between the students. For example, two students could be pointing at Margot, talking about her refusing to take shower. It would show how enemies gossip.
>
> At the end, feeling guilty, ask William to open the door because it was his idea. He threatens the class, but the class is to depressed to be affected by the threats. So, defeated, William, also depressed, decides to open the door. . . .

Seeing William slowly reach for the door. Class crowds in around William. Thunder can be heard. Thunder continues until door opened a little. Thunder stops shortly, then film ends.

By comparison, Rock, who wishes retribution for Margot as a victim, writes:

At the end, I have Margot die because I thought the end was not enough in the story and it seemed was that she lived to see the sun that 1 time and she didn't. . . .

I ended it with her dead on the floor and the room shocked in surprise. She died because she missed what she needed, the sun. It was over for 7 years too long to wait.

During group discussion, Rock had said that having Margot die "would make the kids feel really bad that they didn't let her see the sun, and they also killed her by putting her in the closet." He continues to pursue this notion in his movie.

Rita Mae writes from a more empathetically oriented perspective:

I'd like a boy who tries to stick up for Margot. Margot needed some type of fighting chance in this story. . . .

Have all the children mushing together. A leader in the group slowly opens the creaky door. Everyone sees Margot with her knees drawn up to her chest, crying.

The students never doubt that they and their classmates understood the piece yet developed a variety of differing envisionments, some conflicting. They also assume that their task is to reflect on and more fully develop their ideas, making them more defensible from their chosen perspectives.

When reflecting on his group's discussion, Rock writes:

From our table, many different ending ideas caught my attention. Different thoughts especially on the end varied, but we all kind of agreed it needed something else. From the sun coming out forever to William and Margot being Friends it all varied greatly but the ending was changed from the original story.

About his group's discussion, Manny writes:

Well, our ideas about William varies. Carla believes he's popular
and handsome. I picture him as a mean, chubby, ugly person. We
both agree he bosses people around. I think the fact he does boss
people around emphasices the fact he's a bully, but Carla insists
he's popular.

Our views of the teacher varies also. My group sees the teacher
as a young woman. I see her as an old, forgetful woman. My
argument is the teacher overlooked Margot and I don't think the
class is large. So detached, Margot would naturally stick out. So I
think if the teacher was young, she'd notice Margot's absence.

And Anne-Marie writes:

We didn't agree on anything. Some of the scenes were the same,
but our characters were opposite.

These comments illustrate the ways in which students push one
another's thinking, helping one another expand on and defend their
ideas. They are helped to hone and retain their reactions rather than
forced into agreement. Individual ideas, if they fly, don't get absorbed
into some kind of consensus. The students expect differences, but the
ideas need to "work," and they push one another to make this happen
by providing challenges, agreements, and disagreements.

Day Four

On the fourth day, when the students see the movie, they do so through
the eyes of their own developed envisionments. The students don't expect the movie's interpretation to duplicate their own, but they are as
critical of the director's depiction as they were of one another's; they are
also reflective, open to new possibilities.

For example, Rock writes:

The movie gave a lot of ideas and solutions to mysteries left by the
book. Like how earth was too crowded. Music was used effectively
at many times but I think it was too much. The addition of the girl
who played the role of Margot's friend was much needed. In the
movie you could see Williams jelousy and that was his reason for
being mean to Margot. Also the movie added the extra ending that
was needed because the book just left you hanging.

Dierdre writes:

I thought the end was kind of corny. Margot should have blown up at William instead of walking him inside. The part where they were smelling the flowers was stupid. How did the flowers and grass get there so quick? I liked the girl named Paula.

Carla writes:

The movie was a little like I thought. In the story everyone hated Margo in the movie only William hated her. At the end of the movie they all gave Margo flowers including William because they all felt bad about what had happened. The flowers were a very nice touch to the movie. They all had sun kits which had a visor and suncream in them. She did have one friend Paula.

The students use the quickwrites to prepare themselves for a whole class discussion of their reactions to the movie. They begin by stating their disagreements with the director, but soon move on to discuss their own envisionments, contrasting the two. The students remain open to new ideas, and various perspectives are considered again. It is a lengthy and lively discussion, ending only when Barbara says:

I have to, I'm watching the clock, and I have a concern. Let me talk to you for a minute. We've talked about William and the difference between your interpretations of William in the story and William in the movie. The different Margo in the story and in the movie. Some about the teacher and how she reacted to the class. You've asked some questions about whether the way the story ended was realistic, and/or whether especially the way it ended in the movie. . . . I know it's the weekend . . . but would you just take about ten minutes to . . . step back and imagine that you are Ray Bradbury and that you've just seen this movie. How do you think Ray Bradbury would feel and why? And then, if there's something else you want to say about the story, you can put it at the end of that.

Day Five

In their quickwrites and during the discussion the next day of class, the students respond to the movie in their own ways. To varying degrees, each treats it as *another* rather than *the* other interpretation, just as Barbara had hoped would occur. They treat Ray Bradbury's views similarly.

Rock, who realizes that interpretations are not universal, writes:

I think the book left some unanswered questions that the Movie filled in. Being Ray Bradberry and seeing someone else's interpretation of his own work might make him very critical! Being the author, he already had his own world thought up about the story and so someone else's view (probably much different than his own) might make him upset. He might also get mad because when you watch a movie you not only get the story bet the pictures, which if you had read the bok would have come from your own imagination, not the directors.

Rita Mae writes:

I feel Ray Bradbury would have very mixed thoughts about the movie. Some things I was sure he would of liked and done himself in the movie, and other things I'm not sure he would.

For example, the heat lamps were very futuristic and probably his thoughts exactly. Margot and the teacher were well represented in this. My picture of them was this exactly.

The dialogue in the story was in a Ray Bradbury type also. It matched the story or had the same idea exactly.

Costumes I don't think he would of agreed with. They somewhat dull and grubby looking. They were even older than our style of clothing now.

Scenery he probably would not approve of either. The scenery was imaginative but very dull. I did not keep my attention at all.

And Manny writes:

If I was the author of All Summer in a Day, and I just saw the movie, I would have mixed feelings.

At first glance, I'd be shocked. My ideas of an underground city were not followed, since the movie shows most of the city, a concrete complex, was above ground. . . . Many of the parts of my story, like the time Margot refused to take a shower, were cut from the movie.

But my shock would quickly subside, knowing movie wrights had to change some things, and it wasn't possible for them to include all of my ideas, and I think they did well with what they had available.

Then I would take a closer look. I would look at the characters
and see how they're portrayed.

I would see that my character William was put on charge of others
in the sunlamp scene. The William I created was not responsible.
Would a responsible person lock someone in a closet? I do think the
movie did a good job showing William's jealousy of Margot.

THE ENVISIONMENT-BUILDING CLASSROOM

And so, middle graders learn to develop their own interpretations, elaborate them, and become thoughtful critics—conscious of differences and
distinguishing one perspective from another. The social interactions and
rules of participation within every lesson are wholly focused on what
the students are thinking about, what they know, the ideas they are
developing, and where they situate themselves as learners. We have seen
exemplified, during a weeklong activity, the kind of classroom culture
I described at the beginning of this chapter, where all the participants,
students and teacher alike, believe that literature is thought provoking
and students are competent thinkers. This is the way Barbara's classroom culture works: It is the normal state of affairs.

We have also been able to recognize ways in which the related principles of instruction interweave through and across the interactions and
experiences in this class. From the very first moment through the last,
each and every student in Barbara's class is treated as a natural and lifelong learner, by both the teacher and the other students. It is expected
that each student can and does make sense, and can and will continue
to do so. It is also assumed that any misreadings, misinterpretations,
or weakly founded views can and will be noticed and rethought by
the individual, using ideas from the group to stimulate but not direct
thinking.

As for the second principle, questions are central to all the class experiences. They invite students to reflect on their present envisionments,
explore possibilities, and move ahead. Questions are treated as part of
the literary experience; they provoke interesting discussion and suggest
new possibilities to consider.

The third principle pervades each and every lesson almost by definition. In small group and whole class discussion, as well as in the writing and thinking they do alone, the students' attention is not looking
back toward the understandings they once had but forward, toward the
ones they can develop.

Last, multiple perspectives are considered throughout the unit—those within the class as well as those reflected by the text and movie versions of the story. Such differing perspectives are treated as natural and normal, growing from differing goals, values, experiences, and understandings.

From Barbara's class meetings, we can see that the principles do not operate in a serial manner, one after another. Instead they create an ethos that underlies every moment in her room, shaping the very fabric of the interactions. In supporting students' literary envisionment building, these interactions offer students new strategies and ideas for exploring horizons of possibilities, help them become more aware of others' views relative to their own, provide them with a social context in which to learn to interact with others about those views, and create a sense of ownership for ideas and for learning. How a teacher's actions can foster this is the topic of the next chapter.

6

Strategies for Teaching

People learn how to converse by seeing how it is done and helping one another; they help one another to take turns, bring up ideas, and get on with it. As I am writing this chapter, I am a guest of the Rockefeller Foundation at its villa in Bellagio, Italy. About a dozen other scholars and artists from around the world are also working here, from England, Germany, Hungary, India, Israel, Mexico, and South Africa. We are not only from different parts of the world but also from many different fields. Our life experiences, interests, and immediate concerns are also different, and each one of us has a different expectation about what life in the villa will be like as well as what we ourselves hope to do here. Although all our days are spent in our various offices pursuing our separate projects, we share meals and off-work times, when we carry on conversations. We also make presentations of our work and chat during and after the more formal talks.

We will be here for a month or so and, as we learn to communicate with one another, we are becoming a community. At first it is difficult because our languages and cultures, and thus the communicative traditions we bring with us, differ. In the beginning, at the dinner table and afterward, we make friendly overtures, ask questions, voice statements—but we don't discuss. Not only are our topics of concern different, but our conversational styles and our first languages differ as well. Some people speak easily, often, and rapidly; others listen, think, plan what they will say, and speak slowly. Some overlap their comments onto someone else's turn in a conjoint sharing of ideas, whereas others pause, leaving moments of silence between one speaker and another. Some speak about personal issues; others hesitate to do so with people they have just met. Some comment on others' lives and actions (they gossip), but others consider this impertinent.

At first we don't know how to get on; the "talkers" lead the conversations, opening the topics we talk about and changing them as well, and others become more silent. Miscommunications and misjudgments abound. But we do have daily "meeting" times when conversation is necessary, and we do have essential respect for one another as well as curiosity about what each one thinks, has experienced, and knows. Thus, by our second mealtime, we begin to try to find ways to engage one another. Sandy still opens the conversation, but she asks Elisabeth what she thinks. Elisabeth responds quietly but adds a wonderful new perspective that Sandy and the others had not thought of. Gershon smiles a lot and sometimes nods. He rarely speaks in the large group but does so more easily in groups of two or three. At first, when he speaks at all, it is almost entirely about family and religion, topics that others are happy to discuss briefly but want to move from. Yet Gershon fascinates many in the group when he makes a presentation about his research, in which he combines close exegesis of Greek, Aramaic, and Hebrew writings with recent archaeological discoveries to reexamine some established beliefs about the burning of the second temple in Jerusalem and the exile of the Jews from their homeland. His talk becomes a turning point in his (and our) interaction.

Bit by bit, over time, we create ways in which we, as individuals within a group, can communicate with one another. We find ways for everyone to get into as well as to get on with the conversations. Over time we become a community, forming close relationships and new ways of interacting. After 2 weeks, when a separate 3-day conference is held at our villa (a fascinating conference on the education of women in Africa), we find that we need to adjust to the newcomers, once again being responsive to different conversational styles and new topics.

In a real sense, our group was formed through joint negotiation among the individuals. However, because our unwritten rules for interaction are grounded in what our group members think, do, and say, some aspects of our interactions must necessarily change as new members enter. The interactions are inclusive; people reach out and help one another participate. When we do this, we all learn how to communicate with one another—what to expect, how to draw others out, and how to listen and discuss. We learn about, from, and with one another, as do classroom communities (see, e.g., Santa Barbara Classroom Discourse Group, 1993).

In Chapter 5, I talked about ways in which students think and interact in an envisionment-building classroom. Here I focus on the teacher. The question is, what do teachers do in order to create an environment where thought-provoking and cooperative interactions are usual, and what guides the decisions teachers make? I begin with the kind of social interactions that occur when students and teachers are engaged in activities that have meaning to them, and where the support they offer one another grows from real social and communicative needs. Next, I discuss a way to think about the decisions teachers make when they plan their lessons and as they interact with their students on a moment-to-moment basis. Finally, I turn to goals for assessment in an envisionment-building classroom.

My description of my conversational community in Bellagio is not incidental but critical to the point of this chapter: Literature instruction is an essentially social activity; who the participants are, how they interact, and what they think and know are central. Teachers' decisions about how to help and what to do are also essentially social; they arise from and interact with the ongoing social activity in the classroom. To know what to do requires us to step into and become part of the conversation; it is from a participant's perspective that we best learn about the kind of instruction needed.

COLLABORATIVE SUPPORT IN SCHOOL

In the envisionment-building classroom, students and teacher talk about what they are reading and thinking about. Everyone tries to understand others, to be understood by others, and to think things through for themselves. When people can't quite understand one another, or when participants try to conceptualize or say things that they cannot quite "get out," they help one another.[1] We can think of the help teachers give as help that cannot be planned before the lesson because it is a human response to a meaningful interaction at a particular point in time. This is like the help that pervades our daily lives. Such help is productive because it is contextualized in a real activity. In envisionment-building classes, as with my colleagues in Bellagio, we focus on what we are saying and thinking about, and we support one another in response to as well as through our interactions.

Students need to understand the social genesis of discussion, how to communicate their ideas to others, and how to use discussion productively to develop their own envisionments further. The teacher's support can be critical in helping them learn to participate in such activities. However, teachers' knowledge is often tacit; they aren't always overtly aware of the help they are giving. The help arises naturally out of their pragmatic concerns: They try to make sense of what their students are saying, check that they are understood by others, and suggest ways for them to think about their ideas. The teachers' help is enmeshed in the communication and collaboration (just as it was with my colleagues) and becomes the foundation for the students' development through literature.

In literary discussions, students converse: questioning, agreeing and disagreeing, challenging, helping to push one another's thinking along (Roberts & Langer, 1991). But they need to learn to do this. In the course of their discussion, they help one another, just as we did in Bellagio. Because the teacher is a participant bound up in the social network of communication, even when she or he provides support to a particular student, it becomes part of the group's experience and awareness.

For example, Barbara's discussion of "All Summer in a Day" took place early in the semester, with a new class of students. Barbara felt that some of the students were "strong individuals." They needed to learn to "interact, listen, and wait during discussion, and to be more reflective about their own ideas and to share, discuss, and take in others' ideas." Thus, when the students met as a whole class, Barbara listened to what each student was trying to say and offered support when she thought it might be helpful. Through the support she provided, her students gradually came to understand how they could weave new ideas out of the contributions of other group members, who provide potentially useful feedback and offer possible options.

In a general sense, we can think of the teachers' instruction as providing support for students' participation and also upping the ante—to enrich their ideas. The relationship is a collaborative one in which teachers support students to work through their understandings on their own and with one another but also help when it is necessary. The climate is one of shared communication; teachers serve neither as the sole holders of knowledge nor as evaluators. But they do a great deal of responsive teaching.

Collaborative interactions in envisionment-building classrooms provide two types of support for participants: support that helps people participate in the discussion, and support that helps people think things through. To highlight the teachers' options, I discuss the two kinds of support separately. Then I illustrate how they interact in class. (Teachers don't use these options to plan "lessons." Instead, these are the kinds of options teachers use when they are responding to the social dimensions of participation within an ongoing conversation.)

Supporting Ways to Discuss

As we have seen from my Bellagio experience, when people enter new groups, they often need to make adjustments in the ways they discuss as well as the ways they think. As fairly savvy adults, we were able to do this ourselves—although we did it with difficulty, and some were better at it than others—but students often need a teacher's guidance. Collaborative support for ways to discuss helps students learn the social rules of discussion, such as what is appropriate to talk about in an envisionment-building classroom, how to check that they are being understood, and how to take turns. When teachers support students' ways to discuss, they focus on social behavior (as Barbara did at the beginning of her new semester) in order to help students learn to become participants in thought-provoking literary discussions. One way to do this is to help students become aware of what is appropriate to talk about.

For example, students need to learn that during such discussions it is not appropriate to guess what the teacher thinks is "right"; nor is it appropriate to talk about totally unrelated topics such as last night's social outing. However, it is appropriate to talk about any and all questions and ideas that come to mind in response to the piece. Teachers help students learn ways to discuss by tapping students' understandings, making students aware that their ideas are not being understood and that clarification is needed, inviting students to participate in the discussion and showing them how to "get in," and orchestrating the flow of discussion to emphasize turn taking, connecting with others' ideas, and extending the ideas being discussed. In these ways, the teacher can provide a system of support and guidance that helps students learn how to participate in the envisionment-building community.

Supporting Ways to Think

In contrast, collaborative support for ways to think helps students reason about the topics at hand, sharpen their conceptualizations, and expand their repertoire of ways to explore their concerns; teachers' comments focus primarily on the ideas that students are developing. When teachers support ways to think, they focus on the different ways their students reason about and refine the ideas that are on their minds. They help students become aware of the need to rethink their ideas and suggest ways for them to do so. The support teachers provide here includes help in focusing ideas and narrowing the topic; shaping ideas into a more elaborated, better thought-through, and tighter message; linking ideas from the text, discussion, or personal experience; and upping the ante by offering new and less obvious ways to think about their concerns. Across both types of support, the teacher is never merely a facilitator but a professional and an expert—knowing the discipline and also the students.

EXAMPLES OF COLLABORATIVE SUPPORT ACROSS THE GRADES

Throughout life, individuals need to learn additional ways to discuss and think; the new situations we are confronted with and the people we meet at work, home, school, and the community require this. We are never too old to benefit from help in such learning, nor too young. At school, collaborative support is the mainstay of how teaching and learning "get done"; it forms the fabric of schooling. Let us take a closer look at how this works. I begin with a fairly extensive example from eighth grade and then show parallels at grades 1 and 12.

In Eighth Grade

Let us look at an eighth-grade class in an urban setting. Sandy Bano's students have already spent several months learning to arrive at their own responses instead of providing "right" answers. They are discussing "I Was Born Today," a poem by Amado Nervo (c. 1900/1988). It is a musing on life, thinking of it at its best. The discussion illustrates how a teacher's help can fit into and support the students' moves to better understand. In parentheses, I have described the ways Sandy offers support in this excerpt. She supports students' ways to discuss by tapping students' understanding, seeking clarification, inviting participation, and orchestrating the discussion. She supports their ways to think by focusing, shaping, linking, and upping the ante. Sandy begins by inviting the students to participate in the discussion, guiding them to take turns as well as to share their own thoughts and ideas. When a student responds, Sandy invites more ideas and then helps the students focus and narrow in on what they mean. See how Sandy begins the meeting and how her comments to Tish, Robin, and Lenny act as supports.

Ms. BANO: (*Invite*) What do you think? What is the speaker telling us?
TISH: What the people think like.
Ms. BANO: (*Invite*) Anybody else?
Ms. BANO: (*Focus*) What purpose did he have?
ROBIN: Every day's a new day. Yesterday should be forgotten.
LENNY: He wants to spread peace around the world.
Ms. BANO: (*Focus*) Can you give the line?
LENNY: Not just a line. (*Reads the third stanza*)

Today, every moment shall bring feelings of well being and cheer.
And the reason for my existence,

My most urgent resolve,
Will be to spread happiness all over the world,
To pour the wine of goodness into the eager mouths around me . . .

TISH: It's not true. You might be prejudiced.

Lenny, in response to Sandy's request for greater focus, reads from the poem to illustrate his contention that to him it is about spreading peace around the world. Tish disagrees. Sandy then gives Lenny a chance to respond. In doing this, she is orchestrating, showing the students how to converse with each other—how to connect ideas, how to agree and disagree substantively, and how to use this to extend their thinking. She then invites others to join the discussion, helping Chet focus and Tish clarify her confusing comment so she can be better understood.

MS. BANO: (*Orchestrate*) Lenny, do you want to answer her?
LENNY: They could be friends, and happiness means peace.
TISH: [unclear]
MS. BANO: (*Invite*) Can anyone help them out?
CHET: I don't understand.
MS. BANO: (*Focus*) Who?
CHET: Tish.
TISH: You could be prejudiced and still be happy. That don't mean
    peace.
MS. BANO: (*Clarify*) Can you say it another way?

Tish and Lenny go on to clarify their points; then Sandy recaps what has been said so far and asks for more thinking, inviting ideas and suggesting some ways the speakers might find a focus.

MS. BANO: (*Invite*) So far, Iris says to live for today. Lenny says spread
    peace, but now he says happiness. What else?
BOB: "My only peace will be the dreams of others; / Their dreams,
    my dreams;" . . .
MS. BANO: (*Invite*) How did he get happiness?
TISH: By giving happiness to others, so he then is happy.
MS. BANO: (*Focus*) Ever been in a bad mood and been around a happy
    person and it changed your mood?
STUDENT: And the opposite too, like at a funeral.
MS. BANO: (*Focus*) Look at stanzas 1 and 2. Is he for only forgetting
    the bad, or the good too?
TISH: Both.

There are a number of ideas on the table for discussion. Sandy goes on to help the students move beyond the way they have initially thought about their concerns by upping the ante and offering new and sometimes less obvious ways that they can think about the issues at hand. These occur when, in response to the students' comments, she asks the class for their ideas about the benefits and problems involved in starting over. And, in response to Tish, she wonders why people might benefit from remembering the past.

Ms. BANO: (*Up the ante*) Who thinks it's a good idea to forget and just start over?
CAROL: But if it's really bad, it's really hard to do.
TISH: Yes. But it depends on how bad it is.
Ms. BANO: (*Up the ante*) Is there a time when it's good to remember the past? Is there ever a time when you learn from the past?
TISH: You learn from a mistake and remember not to do it again.

Although Sandy provides a good deal of collaborative support, the students are also active participants—building envisionments and exploring ideas in ways that are decidedly thoughtful. The social structure of the interactions supports literary envisionment building, and the students are learning to become effective participants in discussions of literature.

In conversational situations of this sort, students are given room to work through their ideas with others and alone—moving between public and private selves as their ideas develop. Help can be offered in whole class discussions, group discussions, and one-on-one interactions. The strategies embedded in collaborative support can also be practiced alone, in pairs, and in groups, during activities that involve reading, writing, and speaking as well as other modes of communication such as art, dance, and media. In each of these contexts, students are given opportunities to interact collaboratively with one another and to try things out for themselves. In this way, they experiment with, come to understand, and eventually internalize the ways of talking and thinking about literature that their teachers have modeled for them.

In First Grade

Let us review a brief excerpt from Tanya's class to see how help is offered during the lesson. When Tanya is reading *Sky Dogs* by Jane Yolen (1990) to her first-grade class, some students try to figure out the confusion within the story between horses and dogs.

JAMES: Maybe the mother like [unclear] but his father didn't like dogs.

Ms. WEBER: (*Orchestrate*) Hmmm, that sounds like a good question. Can we think of that question while we're listening to the story?

JEFF: That's the way the author, maybe he thinks it's a big dog that looks like a horse.

JAMES: No, but, it has a longer, it's bigger than a dog and dogs don't have faces like that.

Ms. WEBER: (*Tap understanding*) Does anyone have a thought right now? Matt is just so curious why these look like horses instead of dogs.

JEFF: But I see one that looks like a dog. This is a horse but that looks like a dog.

Ms. WEBER: (*Orchestrate*) Benjamin?

BENJAMIN: One that he said looks like a dog looks like a cow a little. If you've ever seen a cow, a back is like that. It looks, it doesn't have a tail?

Clearly, the children are curious about the confusion. Both of Tanya's comments are attempts to support ways to discuss. In her first comment, Tanya is orchestrating the discussion by giving the students a cue that they should withhold their discussion so early in the story and build up their envisionments a bit more. However, when she sees that they are intent on discussion, Tanya supports their explorations by inviting participation and tapping the students' understandings. She also begins to help them in ways to think by stating the topic of concern, helping them narrow in on the horse and dog problem. When Jeff tries to monopolize the discussion, Tanya orchestrates by calling on Benjamin, who is raising his hand—implicitly reminding Jeff that he needs to let other students join in.

In 12th Grade

Now let's take another, closer look at a portion of Maura Smythe's class discussion of "The Abortion" by Alice Walker (1990).

Ms. SMYTHE: (*Tap understanding*) All right, who'd like to start?

SIKKA: Well, I didn't like her at all. I thought she had the right to have an abortion, and she felt that she needed this. And she said something. She said she chose herself over the child. She wasn't even thinking about what she was doing.

Ms. SMYTHE: (*Shape*) Did she think about it before that, or . . .

SIKKA: I mean, she had thought about it, but she was completely selfish about it. She never, I don't think she looked at what was really happening.

RAINA: I totally disagree. I liked it. I mean, there were parts in it that upset me a lot. Abortion is not really my belief, and she had two abortions, but like, that's not like for me to judge. But generally, I liked the way she personalized the whole thing. She just let you know the situation. And she led you through.

Ms. SMYTHE: (Focus) Did you think she was selfish?

RAINA: I can't, in my opinion, I think she was selfish. She had to choose. Like I've been in situations where you have to choose yourself or somebody else, and the only thing you can do is choose yourself. She like put it that way.

CAROL: I agree with Sikka, because she was just totally, like she wrote she can't imagine another child, even to her husband. He like brought her tea, and she said, "I can't drink that. Take it away." She's just being mean about the whole thing.

CLAUDIA: [unclear] maybe like what she says isn't exactly how she feels, she can't really pinpoint it. Sometimes when people are in that kind of situation, what they say isn't what they mean. Like when you're angry at someone and you don't mean what you say.

Maura begins the discussion by tapping her students' understandings. As in all envisionment-building classes, this initial question invites the students to begin with their present envisionments and move beyond. After Sikka's long comment, Maura asks a question to help Sikka shape her concerns. After Raina disagrees with Sikka, Maura reminds her that she needs to focus on Sikka's comment if she is to disagree, helping her narrow in on whether she felt that the woman in the story was selfish or not. Then other students take over, agreeing and disagreeing with one another and explaining why. Here, they help one another. During all this, Maura observes the discussion, participating only when she thinks that her comment will be helpful.

Teachers at every grade level help students learn more effective strategies for discussing and for thinking. The concerns teachers focus on are responsive to what their students are doing as they consider their own ideas and those of others. In turn, students learn to help themselves and one another by reflecting on the social interactions they have, on the ways their teacher helps them, and on how their teacher gives help to others. Students talk to one another, ask questions, and make suggestions that support others' thoughts and comments. Such interactions mirror what they have learned in everyday life as well as in school. The difference is that in envisionment-building classes, the teachers' and students' comments focus on literature, treating it as a context about which everyone has legitimate ideas and in which ideas are always developing, questions are an essential part of understanding, class is a time to develop understandings, and multiple perspectives enrich developing envisionments.

TEACHING OPTIONS: THE LESSON AS ACTIVITY

The kind of teaching I have described looks very different from that with which most of us are familiar. Teachers sometimes worry about interacting with their students in this manner on a day-to-day basis. "How do I know what to do next?" is a question that may be raised even by teachers who are firmly committed to the instructional principles underlying the envisionment-building classroom. Learning to listen to students' ideas and to base instruction on students' responses is a difficult shift to make. It is easy to find oneself relying on old routines, built up during many years of professional experience. Pre-scripted lesson plans, for example, have been a mainstay of most of our training (and may remain a basis for our performance review by supervisors), yet these plans often work counter to student-based goals. When students respond in unexpected ways, teachers may feel torn, as if departing from the plan involves digressing from rather than delivering good instruction.

Such lesson plans are part of our "old bones"—the internalized routines we have all learned and seen modeled in our own school and graduate course-work experiences. Embedded in our old bones is an idealized conception of what a lesson should look like and how it should proceed. It often begins with a review of what the text "says" (using plot summaries and pop quizzes) and moves to what it "means" (using leading questions that guide students toward predetermined interpretations)—largely inspired by a pedagogy that relies on a hierarchy of questions from literal to abstract (J. A. Langer, 1992; Marshall, 1989).

Yet these old bones are in conflict with a pedagogy in which the primary concern is helping students arrive at their own responses, explore horizons of possibilities, and move beyond initial understandings to more thoughtful interpretations. To feel more professionally confident, we need "new bones." We need a sense of the options available to call upon and use on a day-to-day and moment-to-moment basis in the classroom, in response to what students do and say.

We can take a grand view of the literature lesson as an activity in a Vygotskian (1962) sense (see also Leont'ev, 1981). This means that students are involved in readings, discussions, and other tasks en route to some overarching goal that always involves developing their own understandings of the work or works being read and doing something with those understandings. For example, in Barbara's class, the students planned their own movie of the story they had read and then compared their plans with the movie they saw. Tanya's students discussed their understandings of the lives of the various Native American characters depicted in a number of books. And Maura's students pondered gender issues as portrayed in literature and experienced in life. In each case, the students were given room to develop their own understandings of the pieces they had read and engage in a variety of tasks to help them think about their ideas. Collaborative support was provided along the way, when help was needed. In each case, the lessons were conceived broadly, with teachers treating the various tasks before and after the actual reading and discussion as essential parts of the entire activity, not as separate pre- and postreading exercises.

Such lessons, which can extend across one or many days, can be thought of as including five major sections or options (because each part need not be present in every activity): easing access before reading, inviting initial understandings, developing interpretations, taking a critical stance, and stocktaking. Because together they constitute the entire literary experience, the reading, writing, speaking, and thinking tasks that precede the reading (play, movie) can be thought of as "beginning the literary experience," and everything afterward can be thought of as "continuing the literary experience."

Before I discuss particular aspects of the framework (J. A. Langer, 1994), I want to stress that the strategies I mention are truly meant as options; they are not part of a linear model of teaching, nor are they the only possible strategies teachers can use in thought-provoking lessons. I am suggesting them as ways for teachers to think about their options when interacting with students—as new bones to call upon in place of the old ones.

Easing Access

From the outset, it is important to invite students into the literary experience, providing a signal to them that the primary experience will be a subjective one involving exploring horizons of possibilities rather than an objective one involving maintaining a point of reference. Different teachers do this in more or less elaborate ways. When she starts "All Summer in a Day," Barbara does this by reading to her students, inviting them to focus on their envisionments as well as their eventual movie. Other teachers do this by playing music, reading poetry, or telling stories. But many equally effective signals are quite brief. Tanya, for example, often flicks the lights off and on and steps into the story corner, inviting the students to join her. Cyrus begins by telling his high school seniors, "This is a play you can really get into." After the first week or two of class, Maura usually doesn't need to ease access at all for her Men, Women, and Literature class, because it becomes the expected way of reading. In each case, the students know (or are helped to know) that an experience involving exploring horizons is about to begin.

In easing access, it is important to avoid leading students toward a particular interpretation rather than inviting them to prepare to formulate their own. If it is done in a sufficiently open manner, evoking personal, historical, cultural, or conceptual connections can help prepare them for their coming explorations.

Inviting Initial Understandings

To signal students that their ideas are at the center of the literature lesson, the first questions, tasks, and interactions should tap the understandings students have when they finish a piece. To invite initial understandings, some teachers tell students to jot down their ideas and questions as they read or just after they finish. Other teachers may ask students to jot, draw, or think about and discuss such questions as What's on your mind right now? What did you think when you finished the piece? Is anything bothering you? Barbara asks her students to come up with a couple of good questions for the group to discuss. Tanya often asks if there is something her students would like to talk about. And Maura frequently begins the discussion with, "All right, who'd like to start?" (They know what she is after and get right to it.)

Of course, envisionments change the moment ideas are written or voiced. Thus, it is important to keep initial understandings as provisional and changing and to allow students to move away from them as their ideas develop. Providing time for all students to voice the ideas they had when they finished reading, for example, can inhibit rather than encourage envisionment building by leading them to focus on ideas that have already changed. Initial impressions are always momentary, to be gone beyond. As such, they are expected to be incomplete, imprecise, and open.

Developing Interpretations

Once students have begun to voice their initial impressions, teachers can help them explore and extend their envisionments by questioning and building upon their current understandings. By focusing discussion on the issues the students have brought up, teachers can guide the students as they explore and extend the possibilities within their envisionments. They can be invited to explore such things as motives, feelings, relationships, conflicts, and actions and how these relate to the issues at hand. For example, when Tanya's students are trying to figure out who or what the "sky dogs" are in the story, she helps them extend what they are considering.

SARA: Well, maybe it's just something they've never seen before and they just don't know what it is.
BENJAMIN: I agree with Katie.
OTHER STUDENTS: I agree.
Ms. WEBER: Hmmm? So you think they are seeing something real?
SARA: Yeah, but. . . .

Students can also be guided to reflect on changes that have taken place within a story, or changes in their own thoughts across time. For example, when discussing "The Abortion," Maura asks a question to help her students think about the changes in both the character and the era that might have influenced the woman's decision. Here, she uses changes across time to help them explore and develop a better understanding of the character and the piece.

Ms. SMYTHE: I mean, how is that first one different from the one now?
STACY: She's older now and she's more experienced about it. Probably more legal drugs now, drugs for pain.

Another powerful way to help students develop interpretations is to ask them to take multiple perspectives in exploring the topics they raise. They can use perspectives drawn from within the text, from their own experiences, and from within the class discussion as opportunities to explore rather than curtail their own thinking.

Taking a Critical Stance

As I discussed in Chapter 2, every person engaged in a literary activity sometimes steps out and objectifies the work and his or her experience of it. With their teachers' help, students can do this by examining related issues from the text, history, literature, and life. Teachers can also encourage students to examine alternatives by considering the perspectives of various participants within the text, within the class, and afar, and to use others' perspectives and related possibilities to challenge and enrich their own understandings. Here, generalizing from the text to life, theorizing about the human condition, and contemplating ethical and human issues can become part of the discussion if and when relevant.

For example, at one point early in their discussion of "The Abortion," Maura asks the following of Raina (who was defending the wife's decision) and the other students who had already spoken (who were more sympathetic with the husband):

Ms. SMYTHE: Did anyone . . . (*With a nod to Raina*) You liked the story
   in general. Did anyone like her? What else did you notice about
   the story? This is an issue that people have strong opinions
   about, so maybe that clouded or affected your reading.
BEV: At the end when she was grieving, Holly Monroe, she didn't
   even like know her. . . . Yeah, she said she didn't even know
   Holly Monroe.

Maura's question invites the students to recognize their own biases and to step back from them for a moment and see the characters from other perspectives. At another point, after discussing abortion for some time, she tries to help them consider other critical issues:

This story has a lot of political things about it. Not that women's
issues aren't political, but beyond the abortion thing, it's got lots of
other issues too. What other things did you put question marks by
or comments on as you read?

Here, she invites her students to extend their understanding by looking at social and political issues beyond the one that initially comes to mind. And later, considering the entire unit of short stories they have read, she tries to help her students make connections between the stories and the life and times of today:

If you were trying to judge American culture from these stories,
what would you say about American culture?

Similarly, Barbara helps her students become analytical in response to the movie version of "All Summer in a Day," and later to step into

Ray Bradbury's shoes and become critics from the author's perspective. Tanya also helps her first-grade students step back from their own understandings and objectify the text. After their reading and discussion of *Sky Dogs*, she invites her students to think about the title, saying:

> I would like you to think about why was this story [written] and why in the story did she call it *Sky Dogs*? You might have your idea and everybody might have their ideas.

Taking a critical stance is also where a focus on literary elements and received interpretations becomes relevant. For example, after his 12th-grade class had an opportunity (over several days) to enact, think through, and develop their own interpretations of Sophocles' *Antigone* (see Chapter 1), Kendall encouraged his students to read critical reviews and to read the reviews critically. In such circumstances, discussions of literary and social criticism as well as of the author's craft enrich the students' reflections on their own developing ideas.

Stocktaking

Because literary experiences always need to honor the expectation of changing horizons, we should not look for closure or consensus. As a lesson comes to its end, teachers need to validate the differing interpretations and opinions that have withstood exploration and inspection. This can be done by summarizing key issues that have been raised, noting changes in ideas, acknowledging agreements and disagreements, and pointing out concerns not adequately addressed. It is important to mark the end of the lesson without shutting off thinking, always leaving room for further envisionment building.

The framework outlined here provides a set of "new bones" that teachers can use in thinking about the options available to them. Over time, teachers who are implementing envisionment-building classrooms rely on this framework in different ways. At first they use it to become aware of the options they are using implicitly, then they use the framework more overtly in deciding what to do next, and finally they begin to internalize the options, incorporating them into a more integrated pattern of thoughtful classroom conversation and interaction. Tanya, for example, reflected on how difficult it had been to move from fact-finding questions to those that elicit students' thinking.

> I've thought about the literary experience and how last year it took me, it seemed like weeks ... maybe months. ... But at least for

now, I realize that everything that happened to me last year I must really have internalized because it's not, it doesn't feel chopped up to me now.

[Now] I feel like probably the children are going to be more used to that [developing envisionments and interacting in a thought-provoking way] because I feel that's going to be a more natural part of me and our literary experience. So they are going to be prepared for those things before I even ask them. And yet, I'm wondering, is it necessary for me even to ask a question.

Tanya is aware of changes in her own teaching practices as a result of her own internalization of teaching options. She also realizes that the kind of help she offers her students needs to change based on what they have already learned to do on their own. She perceives her role as providing her students with new and more sophisticated ways to engage in the literary experience.

DOES ANYTHING GO?

With student-based instruction of the sort I am suggesting, people are often concerned that any ideas that come to students' minds will be considered appropriate. Yet this is far from true. The framework of teaching options I have just described summarizes a variety of strategies that teachers use to help students' inspect and reinspect their developing ideas. In these interactions, thinking is stimulated, collaborative help is offered, and learning proceeds. One way to think about the boundaries (what is in or out of "bounds") is that a centrifugal force operates within the social structure of the interactions as students move their gaze outward, always leaving room to explore new horizons of possibilities. However, at the same time, a centripetal force is also operating, counteracting an aimless outward motion and pulling the ideas back inward toward some central core.

Good and reflective thinking is embedded in the social forces within the classroom. Everyone expects to make sense and communicate. As students construct and reconstruct their understandings, the bounds of what is thinkable are set by their own perceptions of the possible. Within the collaborative social setting, the students learn to listen to and reflect on new ideas and take it upon themselves to ignore or reject those that are not working.

Thus, students either incorporate new ideas into their envisionments or abandon them as irrelevant or too far afield. It is the dialectic process of push and pull that provides openness and invites imagination yet maintains an intellectual integrity in the ideas developed within the envisionment-building classroom.

ONGOING ASSESSMENT: EVOLVING GOALS

"But what does this mean for assessment?" I am often asked. "How do I know that my students are learning? How do I grade them? How do I know I'm doing a good job?" These are critical questions that need to be asked, because as the focus shifts from recitation, plot summaries, and single "best" interpretations to the ways in which students reflect on and develop their understandings of the works they read, so too will the criteria that are used to judge effective learning. I address these as they relate to the envisionment-building classroom.

Just as decisions about what to teach need to grow from the particular social context in which the students, teacher, and literary works are centrally located, so too do decisions about what to assess. Context is critical from an envisionment-based perspective, because this view of understanding assumes an inquiring mind and expects good thinking and knowing to be reflected in changing rather than static ideas. Therefore, assessment needs to occur over time, so that ideas have a chance to change and grow. It also needs to take into account a variety of readings of a variety of literary works, since any individual reading activity or task is, in an envisionment-building sense, idiosyncratic. Because the focus is on a particular student at a particular point in that reader's thinking, it permits assessment of the "instant" and is thus potentially relevant for instructional decision making.

In thinking about approaches to assessment, two essential questions need to be asked: What is the assessment for? How will it be used?

The most useful sort of assessment for teachers to use is what I call ongoing assessment. (Peter Johnston [1994] calls a similar process constructive assessment.) This is the type of reflective assessment that students and teachers engage in before, during, and after thought-provoking literature classes. They focus on the thinking students do and did, what they could have done, or what they might try in the future. They also focus on the interactions between the students and the text as they take place in a particular situation, to learn whether something in the social setting is affecting the students' thinking. Ongoing assessment can be very easy and low profile, because it grows from and informs instruction. It can also be a useful feedback mechanism, as much in response to the teaching as the learning, inviting reflection and change.

The most useful ongoing assessments occur when teachers have de-

veloped "new bones," guided by the instructional guidelines and principles I have already discussed. I used to believe that new bones for
instruction were sufficient and that envisionment-building classrooms
would generate new forms of assessment. In some sense this is the case,
but not entirely. Teachers who know that their students are thinking and
learning in new ways usually want something more tangible—both for
themselves and to share with others. I came to realize that just as with
instruction, traditional methods of assessing knowledge are so well-
entrenched that they too require replacement. Merely relinquishing one
kind of assessment is not enough. A replacement on which to base day-
to-day and moment-to-moment interactions in the classroom is also
needed.

Goals for Assessment

A good place to begin in deriving goals for assessment is to review some
of the strategies that effective envisionment builders rely on when they
read and discuss works of literature. Each goal should be thought of as
a conversation starter, with teachers adding and deleting items based
on their own focus at a particular time. The following goals for student
learning are useful at all grade levels and grow directly from the instructional issues discussed in Chapter 5. Each student should be able to:

- share initial impressions after reading
- ask relevant questions about the work being read
- go beyond initial impressions in order to rethink, develop, and enrich understanding
- make connections within and across texts
- consider multiple perspectives within the text and across groups
  of readers
- reflect on alternative interpretations and critique or support them
- use literature to gain understandings about self and life
- engage in ways of reading that indicate sensitivity to other cultures
  and contexts
- use writing as a way to reflect on and communicate literary understanding
- talk and write about a piece in ways that are characteristic of discourse about literature

With a list such as this as a starting point, teachers can begin to reflect
on the contexts in which such strategies might be naturally displayed in
their classrooms. They can develop more specific guidelines or checklists

of their own, with their students or in collaboration with their colleagues. Ongoing assessment will be helpful in the envisionment-building class- room only if it grows from the practical pedagogy that underlies it, creat- ing a seamless unity to instruction, assessment, and classroom interaction. Particularly when the "bones" are new, a listing of goals is helpful because it makes what counts as knowing overt.

A Fairly New Teacher

I close this chapter with some comments from a high school English teacher who began to emphasize envisionment building during his fourth year of teaching. Edward Greer was rethinking the kinds of tests he gave, as well as his instructional approaches. Although most teach- ers who emphasize envisionment building replace end-of-unit tests with thoughtful project activities of various sorts, Edward, who was new to this approach to teaching in addition to being a relatively new teacher, was trying to change the tests he gave. He commented:

> I think my usual approach in my previous years of teaching for literature tests—when I give them, I don't always give them—has been more along the lines of oh, identify where, what town Lenny and George come to. . . . Basically I was testing for what they learned or what they memorized, for little bits of trivia that stuck in their heads, and then I would give them short answers and usually anchored by an essay question that tied things together we talked about in depth. And I realized when I was typing this up, I was testing for their ability to memorize.
>
> What I tried to do on this test was think of the test as . . . a learning experience even while they're taking the test. You're testing two things, how well they know a piece of literature but also their learning. They are showing you the process of thinking about new questions. And so when I was doing my Part I charac- ters, rather than saying, "Who was Tybalt?" . . . I phrased it in a way that they really had to think about as well, "Why was Tybalt in this play?" or "What did Tybalt's presence mean for me as a reader, and why do I think he was there?" It's still showing me that they know something about the plot and what went on in *Romeo and Juliet*, but it's also showing me something different— how they think about the play and what they think about these five characters.
>
> When I got to my short answer, I also said, "Well, let's not test on what Edward wants to hear, let's test on opinion-type questions."

... I'm hoping that's one thing I'm getting across, that I value their opinions, and want them to engage in the play, and it's more important than knowing what act Tybalt dies in. . . . It seems like a very simple switch.

After the test, Jeannie, a student in Edward's class, gave her reaction to it:

Well, it wasn't multiple choice, you really had to know the characters and things they did in the story and understand the story. It was kinda like, well, I think it will help Mr. G. understand that we know more about the story than just fill in the multiple choice, 'cause a lot of kids would a just guessed. This test made you like, think, and just kinda, you get a better idea of the story. I liked it better.

Ben, also a student in the class, said:

Well, you had to describe characters themselves and their individual ways and why they were important, what they did that was so important. I like that about the test because it lets you evaluate the characters themselves instead of evaluating the entire story at once. Instead of having just like questions on who did what to whom and why, like that's just reciting from memory, but this you could actually think about it. The second part, the short answer part, was interesting. You had to do three out of four of them and the questions were a little more intellectual instead of just reciting. You had to think about the relationships of the different characters to each other. . . . It told me consciously what I knew sub-consciously. . . . I changed a few of my opinions on it (too).

After the interviews, we asked Jeannie and Ben if we could play the tape recordings for Mr. G. and received their permission. After listening to the comments, Edward responded:

That was really fascinating. Well, much of what I said before, that didn't change, but I'm surprised at how much in tune students are to what's in front of them. That they, whether they consciously or unconsciously know it . . . they don't value trivial things like matching this to that. They actually see, it sounded like they appreciate having to think on a test. . . . Listening to them, I am becoming to be more convinced that this would be the way to go.

. . . Still, the reaction is, hitting yourself on the head and saying, "Why didn't I do something like this four years ago?" because it seems like a simple adjustment of one's philosophy. But, I guess any adjustment of philosophy is never simple.

I suspect that all teachers who have begun to rethink their teaching would be inclined to agree with that last comment.

NOTE

1. In collaboration with Arthur Applebee, I have conceptualized this kind of collaborative support as instructional scaffolding (e.g., Applebee & Langer, 1983; Langer & Applebee, 1986). However, I have not used the term *scaffolding* here because this term has sometimes been used by others to refer to something more decontextualized and more imposed than what I mean. I would like to stress the essentially social impetus underlying scaffolding. Teachers' decisions are guided by the particular communicative activity, as well as by their overall desire to help students say or do what they themselves have already set out to say or do. Cazden (1988), Rogoff (1990), and Wertsch (1991) provide examples of such support.

7

Literature for Students the System Has Failed

What about students who are at risk, those for whom school has been difficult and at times unwelcoming? Where does literature fit into their experiences? Does the envisionment-building classroom have relevance for them?

I believe that literature education can play a central role in addressing the problems these students face. Every student has had a wide array of literary experiences before ever passing through a schoolhouse door, is familiar with the subject matter (human experience), and knows ways to organize and tell about it. People of all ages come by such experiences through tales they have heard at home, in their communities, and in their places of worship as well as through the personal stories they have told (e.g., Scollon & Scollon, 1981; Witherell & Noddings, 1991; Wolf & Heath, 1993). Through these experiences, students have gained a good deal of knowledge about envisionment building and the structures and strategies underlying literate thinking.

From our earliest years, literature is an essential medium for learning from and communicating with ourselves and others, a way to reflect on our lives, our options, and the human condition. Although there is often a gap between the conventions that govern discourse at home and at school, this gap is less pronounced in literature than in other academic subjects. Students also know and are familiar with expository forms, the kinds that predominate in science and history. However, the conventions these follow in school are different from those used at home, whereas story forms are more similar (J. A. Langer, 1986). For this reason, literature can serve as an important entry into schooling. It can contribute toward each student's development of meaning, sense of self-esteem, engagement in thoughtfulness, and literacy development. In this chapter, I describe a variety of classrooms and activities, each involving students for whom the system has not worked. I do it to provoke thinking about ways in which the concepts I have discussed in the previous chapters can help those who are most in need. Of course, these examples are not meant to represent the full range of students who are at risk, nor to suggest that the envisionment-building classroom is a panacea for their needs. But it is a good place to begin.

THE READING ROOM

The reading room is not a typical classroom but a large, light-filled, oval room next to the library. Instead of desks, there are large tables. Pastel walls, green plants, table lamps, and sofas promise comfort. Numerous shelves overflowing with paperback books invite visitors to browse or curl up with their choice of titles. The reading room is one middle school's setting for remedial reading instruction. Here, students are given individual help in reading on a daily basis. Their placement in the program is based on test scores (below the 35th percentile on the reading comprehension portion of a standardized achievement test) and teacher recommendations. A staff of four reading teachers works as a team. The teachers, school, and district are all highly professional, constantly searching for better ways to engage students in meaningful and enriching learning experiences. Loren Verplank, the most recent addition to the staff, works as a teaching assistant and is completing her master's degree in reading. She wants to implement the principles of the envisionment-building class in her work with remedial reading students. In place of one-on-one student-teacher interactions focusing on what the text says, she offers students in the reading room many more opportunities for interactive student groups focusing on their growing understandings.

Let us look at a discussion of "The King and the Shirt" by Leo Tolstoy (c. 1866/1984). It is about a king who fell ill and could be cured only by the shirt of a happy man. However, the only happy man had no shirt. Prior to this discussion, the students had read and discussed stories and poems together, engaged in shared listening and talking about their questions and understandings, and kept journals to comment on ideas and questions they had about their readings. Loren assigned a group of four students to read the story at home and jot down their questions in their journals in preparation for the group meeting the next day. (This is similar to the procedure we saw Barbara follow with her class.) When Loren had to leave the students (who were seated around a big table) alone for a few minutes, they began to discuss the story on their own.

When she returned, the students asked her to stay in the room but to let them proceed on their own.

Anna opens the discussion. Notice the way she asks an open-ended question that taps the other students' concerns (initially playing the role of teacher). Hoss immediately responds, and the others join in.

ANNA: "The King and the Shirt," uhm, I think we all wrote our questions. I'll start with Hoss. What were your questions or feelings?

HOSS: How could the shirt of a happy man cure the king?

ANNA: Excuse me?

JESSICA: How could the shirt . . .

HOSS: How could the shirt of a happy man cure the king?

JESSICA: How could the shirt of a happy man cure the king?

ANNA: Well, did you read the story?

HOSS: Yeah.

ANNA: How about, where is that part? . . .

CINDY: [unclear] The wise man said if you find a happy man, take his shirt, put it on the king, and the king will be cured.

After some discussion, Cindy asks Anna about her question. Notice the students' interaction, linking their concerns to Anna's and helping to explore possibilities.

CINDY: What do you got?

ANNA: Why is it called "The King and the Shirt"? Even though I know about the shirt and the king he get cured, but I don't understand, like, why didn't they pick something more realistic, you know, like [unclear].

JESSICA: I know, I don't see, like, how a shirt can cure a king.

ANNA: That's just my—go ahead Cindy.

CINDY: I think the ending was really stupid because it goes (*reading from the text*), "The emissaries went in to take off the man's shirt, but the happy man was so poor that he had no shirt." That's the end.

ANNA: He didn't have [unclear] happy man gave the shirt to the king and then the king was happy.

CINDY: But the happy man didn't have the shirt.

HOSS: To get [unclear].

ANNA: I'm saying that and then he gave it to the king then like he didn't have, the happy man didn't have a shirt 'cause he gave it to the king so now he is, like . . . maybe it has to do with the shirt, maybe the shirt is like magic.

JESSICA: I know, I have the question, like, why is it called "The King and the Shirt"? The same idea, or fables 'cause it came from, oh yeah. It was kind of, like, I thought it was boring, just the part where he got cured.

ANNA: I don't understand why somebody would take the time to write a story about a king and somebody's happy shirt to make [unclear].

Notice that the students first discuss their common confusions about the happy man and the shirt, and then Anna explores the possibility of magic. But since her comment, the discussion has been stalled. Cindy tries to help.

CINDY: Anybody else have some comments?

JESSICA: I didn't like the story. . . . It was, like, they didn't really, like, talk about, there's no meaning. It's all really about a king got cured by . . .

SEVERAL STUDENTS: A shirt.

Hoss ups the ante by offering another angle for them to explore.

HOSS: And what happened to the king if he wasn't cured?

SEVERAL STUDENTS: Yeah.

JESSICA: That's a good question! If, like, the author who wrote the, if we could write the author and ask.

CINDY: Is he still alive?

SEVERAL STUDENTS: No, he's not alive.

ANNA: You know, like, if we wrote to the author, we'd have to ask him questions that he could write about, not yes or no answers, because there aren't really yes or no answers to this one.

JESSICA: I know it doesn't really answer a question. Any other thoughts?

ANNA: In my opinion, I don't think there is, like, not too many more opinions.

Because they seem to have reached a stalemate, Jessica steps in to help, suggesting that she read the story aloud to gain ideas. The students seem to see read-aloud as a time to move their envisionments along. Notice Jessica interrupting her reading to comment on her thoughts.

A king once fell ill. "I will give half my kingdom to the man who can cure me," he said. But no one knew. Only one of the wise men said what he thought would cure the king. "If you can find a happy man, take his shirt, put it on the king, and the king will be cured." [I think, like, the king might have, like, problems and he might be more happy if he takes a happy man's shirt.] *The king sent his emissaries to search for a happy man. They traveled far and wide throughout his whole kingdom, but they could not find a happy man. There was no one who was completely satisfied: if a man was rich he was ailing; if he was healthy he was poor; if he was rich and healthy he had a bad wife; . . .*

Anna continues the reading.

or if he had children they were bad. Everyone had something to complain of. Finally, late one night, the king's son was passing by a poor little hut and he heard someone say, "Now God be praised. I have finished my work, I have eaten my fill, and I can lie down and sleep. What more can I want?" The king's son rejoiced and gave orders that the man's shirt be taken and carried to the king, and that the man be given as much money as he wanted. The man's emissaries went in to take off the man's shirt, but the happy man was so poor . . .

Several children, giggling, chime in to complete the sentence, and the dialogue continues.

SEVERAL CHILDREN: *that he had no shirt.*
HOSS: He was really [unclear] as much money as he wanted. . . . He was just praying for God and then all of a sudden [unclear] his happiness.
CINDY: But the guy didn't have a shirt to take off.
ANNA: That was my other question. Why did it turn out the man have no shirt?
CINDY: Because he's too poor.
ANNA: But, I'm saying could it, when they couldn't find any other shirt and when they came to this man why they came to this man if he didn't have it either?
JESSICA: Because (*sighing*) . . .
ANNA: You know what I mean? Like, they trying to find one.
JESSICA: He's the only guy they could find.
CINDY: He is the happy man.

The students take ownership for the entire discussion, starting it, providing support for their developing understandings, keeping the envisionment building going, and closing the meeting. This group of "remedial" readers is engaged in highly literate activities: entering stances, exploring horizons of possibilities, and using the social-interactive context as well as the text to explore ideas in their attempt to move their understandings along. Unlike so many students who have been taught to be "poor" readers—those taught to search the text for "the" meaning—these students know how to use the text for their own purposes: to spark their ideas, answer their questions, and develop their envisionments.

Throughout the discussion, the students adhere to the principles underlying the envisionment-building classroom (described in Chapter 5), treating one another as thinkers and their meeting as a time to explore ideas, develop understandings, and go beyond. They know that in literary communities they need to listen to and share ideas, engaging in a collective search for meaning. Afterward, when Anna was asked how she knew what to do during the discussion, she said, "We have done this with Ms. Verplank," suggesting that they had internalized the social rules of the reading room.

Clearly, the students know that in their work with Loren, understanding does not involve going after a "right answer" but working with the ideas and trying to make sense of them. When the session ended, the students had done a good deal of thinking but had not really worked through their essential problem. They are aware of this. For homework, in her journal, Jessica writes, "I think it [the story] is kind of good now because we discussed it and I sort of started to understand it more because it is like . . . I just liked it because we all discussed it because I like to hear other people's thoughts."

This discussion took place in May. Loren's beliefs about "knowing" as well as her teaching routines had changed a great deal as she began to emphasize envisionment building, as had her ideas about teaching remedial readers. We can see reflected in her students' interactions the supportive social context she has created, one that guides students' thinking and gives them room to be curious and to use all the clues at their disposal to help them make sense. At the end of the year, Loren describes her own experiences:

> This has been a wonderful year. . . . I think in a different way of teaching now. . . . I'm always going to be searching, there is no right answer. . . . I want the kids to think . . . keep asking questions. . . . We tend to lower the expectations with remedial readers . . . extended meaning is seen as extra credit. I try to stretch their opinions.

A NINTH-GRADE ENGLISH CLASS:
STUDENTS WITH SPECIAL NEEDS

Let us turn now to a ninth-grade English class. It is a small class (nine students in September, dwindling to six in May), and all the students have been identified as having special needs. Some of the students have been in self-contained special education classes; others have been mainstreamed but receive extra support from a specialist. One student is confined to a wheelchair because of muscular dystrophy; two are tentatively diagnosed as having attention deficit disorder; another is considered hyperactive and being medicated with Ritalin. All are scheduled for remedial reading in addition to this English class. Although it is a small group, the class meets in a regular classroom used for groups of 20 to 30 students during other times of the day. When this group meets, their desks are often arranged in a circle. Jane Robbins, the teacher, uses one of the student desks for herself during class time.

Jane is a veteran teacher who is also the high school English chairperson. Although, as chair, she can teach any class of her choosing, Jane says that she had an "itch to see what could happen with a class like this if a teacher moved beyond the skills and drills approach" to an environment where the literary experience would be encouraged. She believes that the students are capable of engaging in richer literary experiences than they have previously had an opportunity to engage in.

Jane works hard to "create a community of trust, not just of others, but ourselves and our ideas" within this classroom. She also works hard trying to develop her own new bones—to create her own ways of offering the support and encouragement needed to help these students become more active thinkers. Her students are reading *Journey to Jo'burg* by Beverley Naidoo (1986). It is about a sister and brother, ages 9 and 13, who are growing up in rural South Africa when it is still under apartheid. Their baby sister takes ill, and they begin a 290-mile walk to Johannesburg to find their mother, who works as a live-in domestic. The story is about the dangers and indignities the children face on their journey, and the way their mother shows that she cares about them.

Jane begins by developing a list of open-ended questions that she hopes will invite her students to step into the story. For example, she asks them, "How would you feel if you were Naledi or Tiro and the bus driver shouted at you like that?" Their responses, as written in their journals, include:

No, I'm not stupid. Who do you think you are telling me I'm stupid?, etc. (Roger)

I would tell that person they must be stupid. No one yells at me, because I don't know anything about this [segregation], and I'm not from around here. So you must be the stupid one to talk to me like that. (Kate)

If I were the children, I would probably say something to him [the bus driver]. But the children probably feel bad. (Bonnie)

I think that the white people are mean to the black people. I don't think that where they are is a nice place because the whites are mean to the blacks. I would feel sad and mad. I would tell the bus driver to shut up. I would say that I'm not different than whites. (Paul)

Jane then uses these journal responses as a basis for discussion in class. Paul first shares what he has written (with no elaboration), and Kate picks up on it.

KATE: That's exactly true. Just because you're colored, your skin is a different color, doesn't mean that you're different inside. It gets me mad when white people call them niggers and spics.
Ms. ROBBINS: Evan?
EVAN: I'd be really upset. It just wasn't fair.
Ms. ROBBINS: Brandee, what do you have?
BRANDEE: The children must feel bad. They might think it's their fault.
KATE: Yeah. The children probably thought it was their mistake.
ROGER: I wrote, "I think I would cry. I think I would be confused, I don't understand why all this separation, and aren't I as good as those other people? This is an ugly world. All I would want to do is run away."

These are rich and provocative responses from students who too often are asked only to explain vocabulary or literal meanings. But the students are learning what counts in the class discussion Jane is trying to support. They have begun to think about central issues and are learning to communicate with one another about them.

The next excerpt comes later in the lesson, when the students are discussing how the two children and their mother finally meet after a long separation. The students collaborate to explore possibilities and build envisionments.

BRANDEE: Is she a maid?
EVAN: Yeah.

KATE: She's dressed like a servant, like a slave, actually.

PAUL: Why can't the kids stay with their mother?

KATE: Maybe they [the employers] are prejudiced.

PAUL: But why can't she just keep her kids there too? She could watch them while she watches their kid.

ROGER: 'Cause that would distract her.

PAUL: But the kids could help her do stuff.

Throughout this part of the school year, Jane is struggling with ways to help her students think more deeply about the critical issues they raise. She finds the instructional framework (see Chapter 6) that describes decision-making options—easing access, inviting initial understandings, developing interpretations, taking a critical stance, stocktaking—helpful. She says:

I think that as far as following students' agendas, student thinking rather than my own, that is something I'm much more conscious of now and can allow it to happen. Not *allow* to happen, I mean I can *work* to make it happen.

LOVELL MIDDLE SCHOOL: A POOR URBAN COMMUNITY

Sandy Bano teaches in an urban school where 20% of the seniors do not graduate with their class because they do not pass state-mandated examinations; approximately 40% of the students do not graduate at all. About a third of the students are from families below federal poverty guidelines. Approximately 54% of the students are white, 42% African American. The school serves smaller percentages of Asian and Hispanic students and an increasing number of students from India, Afghanistan, and Pakistan. (In Sandy's eighth-grade class, the ratio is 20% white and 80% African American, and all are considered "below-average" readers.) The district provides little support for teachers' innovations, although it does want to improve student performance and is in the process of initiating magnet schools and school-based management.

The desks in Sandy's classroom are arranged in rows, facing front. There is a pleasant clutter, with books and papers piled haphazardly on the floor, but the walls and shelves are relatively barren. Sandy wants to help her students read and think about literature from an envisionment-building perspective: "I had taken my teaching of literature for granted and assumed the 'old way' was the 'only way.'" She is working to engage her students in active discussion: "Everyone's opinion counts." The students keep response journals and hold small group as well as whole class discussions.

Let us look at Sandy's class of below-average readers as they read and discuss "The Rocking Donkey" by Joan Aiken (1959/1988). It is a story of a rich and wicked stepmother, a very lonely girl, and magic. On the first day, students take turns reading the story aloud and then meet in small groups to make notes about questions that they might discuss later. They spend the rest of this and the next class meeting discussing their questions and exploring the possibilities raised by the story. Sandy introduces the story by "easing access."

Ms. Bano: We're going to read a story called "The Rocking Donkey." Umm, I'm ... if you're the type that cries with *Bambi* when you watch it, you'll like this one. This is a very, very sad story. (*Students are snickering*) I always want to cry when I read this story. Maybe you guys are tougher than I am, but I cry.

Ron: I'll read.

Ms. Bano: All right. Everyone can have a turn to read who wants to.

When the students discuss their questions in the whole group, Sandy takes notes and puts the questions on the board for use the next day. When they meet the second day, she immediately reminds them of their discussion and invites them to continue developing their ideas.

Ms. Bano: I wrote them [the questions] all down on the board this morning just so we could remember what happened in class yesterday, and I even put down some answers [some things they had discussed]. Nesha wanted to know how stepmother treated Esmeralda while father was alive. . . . We really didn't focus a lot on that yesterday. Anybody want to talk about it a little bit more?

A number of students: (*Answering at once*) Yes. Yeah.

Koko: The father probably woulda got mad if she was treating the stepdaughter wrong. Probably woulda divorced her.

Nesha: She would probably have divorced him.

Ms. Bano: All right. So why the change now?

Nesha: Because she probably missed the stepfather. She should have treated her better. Because, it's, like, Esmeralda is part of the father. And she was married to the father and should have treated her better.

Ms. Bano: Okay, anybody else?

When the students have no more to say about a topic, Sandy moves on to another question but always leaves room for them to return to an earlier topic and to make links with issues discussed earlier.

Ms. BANO: All right, then, Iris mentioned she wanted to know why Mrs. Mitching acted like she was rich but treated Esmeralda like she was poor.

NESHA: She's probably not ashamed, she just, like, when she went there in the brown dress, she was, like, she's a little too dirty, "going to ruin my image." She's thinking more about herself than she is the little girl.

Ms. BANO: That's a good point. All right, so we've got (*writing on the board*) . . .

KOKO: Then that, right there brings everything back to the dress, 'cause, like, she's got to be ashamed of her, right? Because she only got one dress that she wears when she goes out. And then the brown dress she always wears.

The students discuss this issue a bit longer, and Sandy begins to invite others to join in the conversation, supporting them in ways to discuss and ways to think.

Ms. BANO: Okay, then Lanita said (*referring to the blackboard*) maybe she didn't want the stepdaughter, maybe she just wanted the father. Anybody else want to agree, disagree?

CONRAD: I don't think so.

Ms. BANO: All right, why not?

CONRAD: 'Cause she didn't treat her right. She could [unclear].

KOKO: She's ashamed of her.

Ms. BANO: Okay, Ron?

RON: What?

Ms. BANO: What do you think? . . . Pick a point. Say something today, please.

RON: I'm thinking.

Ms. BANO: Okay. When you think of something, let me know. Well, Iris.

When the students recycle ideas they have already discussed, Sandy reads part of the story to them again and suggests that they think of differences between the ending of the story and how things had been earlier. This provides the students with new possibilities to consider: "Remember, they're just possibilities we can think about." (Sandy continues to jot students' comments on the board.) She also supports ways to think by asking open-ended questions for the students to consider, in response to the issues they have already raised.

Ms. Bano: (*Reading what students had already said*) "She could have snuck out of the house. She could have ridden the donkey." Now, what about this riding the donkey and never being seen again?

Koko: Well, she could have never been seen again.

Ms. Bano: (*Writing*) She could have never been seen again.

Nesha: She could have run away.

Ms. Bano: All right.

Koko: Well, both of them could of, she could of took the horse, I mean the donkey.

Ms. Bano: Okay. Now, what do you think really happened? When it says, "Never was seen again."

Lenny: She left. She ran away.

Ms. Bano: She left, she ran away. With the donkey, ran away. All right.

(*A number of students are mumbling*)

Ms. Bano: (*Writing*) Ran away. Are there any clues earlier in the story to point to the fact that she might run away?

Koko: Yes. The way her stepmother was treating her. She didn't have no clothes, she had no friends.

Lenny: She had no toys.

The students suggest many reasons that Esmeralda might want to run away. The discussion continues at length in this fashion, exploring alternatives and then looking for evidence. Sandy records the students' suggestions on the board, revisiting them later in the discussion. The students all agree that Esmeralda has good reason to leave home (to find friends, stop mom's bad treatment, find happiness). Then Sandy asks them to think about what Esmeralda could have done instead of running away (a question that taps students' knowledge). See how many more students enter the discussion as it progresses.

Lanita: She could have killed herself, she could of . . .

Nesha: You know, like some neighbors could have moved next door.

Ms. Bano: Are you saying this along with the suicide?

Koko: No, she could of stayed there and tried to find happiness, instead of running away.

PIERRE: She could have jumped through the window.

Ms. BANO: All right. Before we go on, class, Pierre, you hang on to yours too, 'cause I want to talk about this one a little bit before we go to another one. Class. What about the suicide? Let's do the same with this. We said there were possibilities because of the treatment, possibilities that she could have run away. Are there possibilities or any clues in the story to say she'd commit suicide?

LANITA: No. Not really.

PIERRE: I'm saying after she went through the window, she could of fell or something.

LARRY: Don't you think the donkey would of saved her if she woulda fell?

PIERRE: But it's dead [inanimate], not alive.

MIMI: 'Cause she's imagining this.

Ms. BANO: Is she imagining it so she is really gone, or is she imagining that she's gone?

MIMI: Probably dreaming. Yes, she's dreaming that she was on the horse, took it out the window, sat it down when they was on the window ledge, jumped.

(*Many students talking at once*)

Ms. BANO: Class, hang on a minute. Pierre said he thinks they all lead up to one thing. What is that?

MIMI: We said that already.

BOYS: She died.

The discussion continues, with students discussing this possibility, looking for clues in the text as well as arguments they can muster and discuss with the others. All in all, it is a very literate discussion for students who have scored between the 6th and 46th percentiles on their multiple-choice standardized reading tests.

In her end-of-year notes, Sandy wrote:

Using response journals has enhanced classroom discussions because the students are given time to think about a piece of literature before they speak. . . . The students aren't "put on the spot."

About students working in pairs or groups, she noted:

Then by the time we discuss in a whole classroom situation, the students are usually very comfortable with the topic at hand and therefore discuss freely. . . . I have been surprised by how trusting they've become of me and each other. . . . The class has also learned that I won't give or necessarily even know the "right" answer. It was hard for me at the beginning of the school year not to answer a question because I was uncomfortable with the silence. I have gotten much better with that and it happens less frequently because the students know it has to come from them.

JUNIOR HIGH 306: BILINGUAL AND ESL CLASSES

Junior High School 306 is in an extremely poor section of a large urban center. The neighborhood has always been poor; it is home to the most recent and poorest immigrants from around the world. It is always in transition, with more settled groups moving on, making way for new waves of settlers. It is a neighborhood of dualities: filled with hard-working people with a love of family and country of origin, yet plagued by drugs and violence. Crack vials crunch underfoot in the school yard. Knife fights are common, and guards stand at the schoolhouse door and in the corridors, communicating with one another on walkie-talkies in their attempt to keep unwanted visitors out and protect those inside. They are not always successful. Recently a student was stabbed to death in the corridor on the way to class.

The statistics are not encouraging. At this school, 83% of the students have been categorized as low income; about 50% have part-time jobs. It is one of the lowest-achieving schools in the city.

Carlotta De Vito, an English as a second language (ESL) teacher, Herlinda Suarez, a bilingual teacher, and Rosa Ramirez, a former teacher at the school who returns regularly to work with the students, have been exploring ways in which literature can serve as an avenue to literate thinking and academic success for students whose first language is not English and who may have been living in the United States for only a few months or a few years. All the students in the class have been categorized as having limited English proficiency and are therefore required to select either bilingual or ESL for special assistance in language and literacy. The majority are recent immigrants from the Dominican Republic.

Every culture has a literary tradition that students know and can call upon. It is a strength through which they can come to understand their own and others' human experiences, ways of communicating, and forms of literacy. To build on this knowledge, the students were engaged in making a collection of stories drawn from their own lives. They could tell the stories as they had heard them or change them as they liked. They could even compose their own. The goal was to publish a book of stories in English and Spanish for other bilingual and ESL students to read. This was no easy task and, with stops and starts, took them the entire school year.

First the students interviewed their family, friends, and neighbors to locate stories they wished to tell. They practiced telling the stories aloud, as close to the original versions as possible. At school, the students met in groups to hear one another's stories and critique what they heard. With support from the teachers, they learned to focus on aspects of the content (e.g., Is all the information you need to understand the story included? Is there anything that needs to be made clearer?); genre (e.g., Is this the way your grandmother (the story's original teller) would have told it? What could be changed to make it more like the kind of story it is?); and organization (Does anything need to be changed at the beginning, middle, or end? Can the reader follow the train of thought?). After tape-recording their stories, the students wrote them in their language of preference, and after these were "polished," they translated them so that there was a Spanish and an English version of each story.

Producing the collection involved speaking, writing, and reading in both languages, as well as polishing the prose. The teachers offered support as needed. Throughout the year, the students read and told many stories, each involving the students in exploring horizons of possibilities and making connections to their own stories. Let us look briefly at one small group meeting in Ms. De Vito's class. Rene is working on his story, and the others are providing feedback. Like almost all the students, he writes his story in Spanish, and the group discussion is almost entirely in Spanish, except for occasional shifts to English. The following is a translation of the actual discussion.

RENE: Once upon a time I used to live in Caracas, Venezuela, about four years ago. That was in 1989. One time my father arrived from work, from, from El Junquito [the town where the father worked]. And when my father arrived, he asked me to bring him a cup of coffee. But my mother found this very strange. Because he always goes to my mother to greet her, but this time he didn't go, he went straight to bed and turned the TV on. And he started to watch "Sabado Sensacional" [a popular TV show in Spanish].
(Sonia and Clara giggle)
RENE: And when I took the cup of coffee to him, he had fainted in the bathroom and was yellow. We thought that he was dead, was dying. But we took him to the Red Cross and also, and they had to change one of his lungs. And when they were going to let him,

when they were going to let him go, Dr. Longaniza . . . he said
that he [the father] was going to give us [unclear] to have problems, and if we had problems, that we should take him to the
hospital. Again, again, when they let my father go, we took, we
took him home. And that same day a thief came in our house. My
father was, he was sleeping. But since I saw him, my mother
woke him up . . . and my father had a 22, 38, and a Magnum. But
my father took the baton that police persons use and he took the
22. When my father caught the thief, he said to him, he hit him
with the baton between, between his forehead . . . the thief, from
the thief. And then my father shot the thief with four bullets, two
in the arms and two in the legs. And my father told him freeze or
I'll shoot you. . . . And when my father was fighting I called the
police, the firefighters, the armed forces. After all of that, they
took the thief to the hospital. And then to jail. They took my
father, we took my father to the hospital in the morning because
Dr. Longaniza said we should take him for two weeks. And
when my father left there, they told my father that the lung was a
Chinese lung. To him, to himself, the same day that my father
was teaching me karate, a thief came in and when we were going
to bed at midnight the thief came in and my father he, he fought
him with karate and when I saw him fighting, I called the police.
Only because the man knew karate I didn't have to worry. And
when everyone woke up I told them whether they, whether they
wanted to bet and everyone bet against my father and I won a lot
of money because my father won. My father broke one of his
arms, a leg, and the, and the bone in the middle.

(*Clara and Sonia erupt in laughter*)

RENE: After everything took place, the police came and took him both
to jail, but they let my father go after, after two weeks, and when
they let him go, my father had the lung of a priest and instead of
going out to play in the street on Sundays he would go to church,
but at least he wasn't violent. And now he doesn't have to fight.
That's it.

MS. RAMIREZ: (*Giggles*) Okay. (*Looking at the students*) What do you
think? And you [Rene] too, what do you think yourself? Now,
that you have read it, it's been a while that you hadn't thought
about the story, and now that you have read it, what do you
think, Rene?

RENE: [Unclear] because I don't know what happened there.

MS. RAMIREZ: And what do you think about what he said . . . like a
little mixed up?

CLARA: A bit.
RENE: At the beginning.
MS. RAMIREZ: And what can be done to rectify that?
RENE: No, that I didn't put what was happening, I think I forgot [last
    time the students had suggested he provide more information at
    the beginning]. . . . I had to put that a thief was coming in.
MS. RAMIREZ: Yes.
RENE: It was going to come in tonight.
MS. RAMIREZ: Yes.
RENE: I didn't do it, I forgot to put it in.
SONIA: And that, you didn't put, see you later, alligator.
CLARA: You left many small things.
MS. RAMIREZ: But come here, what we said now about Clara's story
    [the story they had just discussed]. Do you remember what she
    needs to do now is to make it more like a story, and less like a
    personal account, right?
CLARA: Yes, you have to put the little things that you took out.
RENE: No, no, I put the freeze.
CLARA: Which was very funny.
RENE: I put the freeze or I'll shoot you
CLARA: That was cute, right? That gave it a bit of . . .
SONIA: Seasoning.

The students then suggest to Rene that the story seems mixed up. In
this discussion, they focus primarily on the content. Clara suggests that
Rene needs to work "on the problem" and also on what happens. They
point out that the part about the two lungs needs to be made clearer,
and that the part about the thief is hard to follow. They also remind Rene
that it is too long and complicated and suggest that he cut the part about
the thief. They tell him that they like the humor he added. During the
rest of the year, Rene took his story through several more rewrites, participated in other meetings like this one, and translated and polished
the story on his own and with help from his classmates. By the end of
the year, Rene's story looked like this:

Mister Lung (Señor Pulmon)

Four years ago, in 1989, when I lived in Caracas, Venezuela, my
father worked in a place called Junquito. One day, when he
returned from work, he went to bed and sent me to get coffee. But
my mother knew something happened because he didn't hug her
as usual. So we took the cup of coffee to him, and when we got

there he was on the bathroom floor, fainted. We called the Red Cross.

They checked him at the hospital, and told us he needed a new lung. When Dr. Longaniza came out of the operating room, he told us we were going to have problems because it was a cop's lung he had replaced the bad lung with. Then we took my dad back to the house and went to sleep because it was late at night. But that same night, a thief broke into the house. I woke up and saw the thief, so I called my father and told him. My father reached for a 22, a 38, a magnum, and a nightstick. Then he took the night stick and hit the thief in the middle of his head. My father told him, "freeze or I'll shoot." Then he shot him four times, two in the arms, two in the legs. When my father was fighting I called the cops, the firefighters, and the Army, and they called an ambulance. After all of that the cops took the thief to jail, after a stop at the hospital. And in the morning we took my father to the hospital, because Dr. Longaniza said that if there was a problem, to bring him back to the hospital.

When they let my father out two weeks later, the doctor told us my father had a Chinese lung. The day my father was teaching me karate, another thief came into the house. At midnight, the thief came in the window and my father saw him. He started fighting karate with the thief. The stinking thief knew karate too! But I wasn't worried. All the people who lived nearby woke up, and everybody bet against my father. So I won lots of money because my father beat him up. My father broke the thief's arm, leg, and neck.

After all that happened the cops came and arrested both of them. But they let my father out after two weeks. When they let him go, Dr. Longaniza changes his lung once more. This time it was a priest's lung and instead of hanging around on the street, on Sundays he goes to church. At least he is not violent anymore and doesn't need to fight.

Toward the end of the year, Herlinda Suarez's class read "Flight" by John Steinbeck (1989). It is about the Torres family, a mother and her three children aged 12, 14, and 19, who have a small farm on a cliff overlooking the ocean in Monterey, California. The father died some years before, and Pepe, the eldest son, begins to take on responsibilities for the family. But when he goes to town on an errand, he gets into a fight and kills a man. The story is about his flight and eventual death.

When reflecting on the school year, Herlinda said that 8 months before, the students would have been complaining, resisting the material.

"This story is too long," they would have whined. "Are you crazy, we can't read all that." Herlinda explained:

They didn't think they were capable of reading more than a page. Now they say, "Let's read and finish it." And they know how to build ideas and talk about literature in different ways than earlier.

The explorations of literature (theirs and others') that had gone on throughout the year gave the students a way to step into Steinbeck's story and make it their own.

BUILDING ENVISIONMENTS

In the school experiences I have described in this chapter, the principles underlying the envisionment-building classroom prevail. The students are treated as if they can and will make sense of the material they read and write. Questions are considered a normal part of the experience. Class meetings are a time when ideas are developed and collaborative support is offered, and multiple perspectives are expected. The students participate in literate thinking as a matter of course, pursuing their ideas with their own sense of purpose.

The students we have read about in this chapter are at risk for different reasons, and their special classes have different labels. (Perhaps special class assignments themselves require rethinking, but they are a reality in many localities, and it is the pedagogical theory that underlies classrooms of all sorts that I want to stress here.) However, in the envisionment-building classroom, all the students behave like the adept language and literacy learners they are outside of the school context, and they also learn to use the strategies associated with "schooled literacy." They learn the literate thinking strategies that are most often associated with academic success.

Loren Verplank's reading room students were also in Barbara Furst's English class (see Chapter 5). In this English class, it was almost always impossible to identify which students were scheduled for the reading room and which were not. They helped and gave help. They asked questions and sometimes did not understand things. They used the social context of the classroom to gather ideas and develop their envisionments.

Some students were quiet, especially at the beginning of the year, or when a particular piece was being discussed. This was their idea-gathering time, a time to listen to the content and discourse and notice the ways of thinking that marked discussions of literature. And when they were ready to participate, they did so. Their contributions melded into the ongoing flow of ideas that constituted the group's exploration and the individual's development of interpretations.

This, I think, is why it is so difficult to discern the "remedial" readers after they have participated in envisionment-building classrooms for some time. In these classrooms, students call upon language and literacy strategies and ways of thinking that they know and use—in a context where what they know is sanctioned.

8

Learning Literary Concepts and Vocabulary

From what I have discussed thus far, it might seem as if I treat literary understanding as a *way* of thinking without an accompanying focus on *what* to think about. Although I want to stress the contribution of literary experience to intelligent thought, thinking never happens in isolation: What to read about and why have always been major concerns in literary education. In this chapter, I address a major concern that teachers raise when attempting to embrace a more student-based view of instruction: How do students learn the technical concepts and vocabulary that underlie literary texts (such as literary elements and structure)?

LITERARY KNOWLEDGE IN
THE ENVISIONMENT-BUILDING CLASSROOM

Whenever I speak with teachers about student-based approaches to the teaching of English, they always raise a question about the place of traditional knowledge. Many fear that when the focus turns to students' thinking, something called "knowledge" (literary concepts and vocabulary) has no place. From my perspective, nothing could be further from actuality. In the classes I have discussed in previous chapters, when students think about and talk about literature, literary knowledge is used and studied. This is apparent in the language and concepts students use to talk about what they have read. The difference is that in a traditional curriculum, such knowledge is isolated and predetermined, whereas in envisionment-building classes, it is organic, growing from the students' interactions with and explorations of literary works.

Literary knowledge is evident in the envisionment-building classroom in what students think about and how they express their ideas. The teacher who listens to what students are attempting to express, and how, becomes sensitive to their knowledge growth and can help support and guide it in significant ways. There is no separation between knowledge and strategies. Rather, literary knowledge becomes part of the seamless fabric of ongoing thought and language within the classroom community.

Literary knowledge is an integral part of how students build and develop envisionments. Literary language and concepts creep into almost every discussion in which individuals are creating and exploring their own understandings in response to a literary experience. They constitute the ideas that come to mind as students form, reflect on, and defend their understandings. Therefore, envisionment-building classrooms are not only environments where responses develop and interpretations are built but also places where technical concepts and vocabulary are learned and taught. This occurs as an outgrowth of the ongoing activities and interactions the participants engage in. My notion of technical concepts and vocabulary is related to what Vygotsky (1962) calls scientific, as opposed to spontaneous, concepts. These are learned as a result of schooled experience, during activities that provide ways to try things out and develop a sense not only of what the concepts mean and when to use them but also how they work.

The kinds of knowledge that emerge in envisionment-building classrooms are also responsive to changing concerns within the field of English and the world at large, leaving room for various readings and interpretations to focus on current cultural and theoretical concerns. Such issues arise as a natural part of the humanely provocative literary experience, as individuals and the group explore horizons of possibilities and develop and rethink an array of their own and others' interpretations.

In this chapter, I look at some of the specific ways in which literary knowledge is used and learned in envisionment-building classrooms. Although in such classrooms formal aspects of literary language and concepts are never the overt focus (as they often are in traditional literature lessons), they keep cropping up in the discussion that occurs as participants explore, explain, and defend their understandings.

This is evident in the following example from Marty Bickle's seventh-grade class. The class is reading a series of poems about personal feelings and relationships. After reading "The Secret Heart," a poem about relationships between a father and child by Robert P. Tristram Coffin (1939), the students meet in small groups to raise questions about the piece. One group takes responsibility for discussing the poem more fully among themselves, in order to serve as key discussants during the class meeting. From their discussion, it is apparent that Sarah disagrees with another student and uses her knowledge of metaphor to reopen a discussion about the entire piece. When the students continue to discuss their understanding of the poem, technical concepts and vocabulary such as metaphor, literal meaning, and symbolism are introduced into the discussion. Some students, such as Stu, do a more surface reading and seem less familiar with the notions underlying the concepts than their classmates. However, they learn through in-context experience—by listening to the conversation, questioning their classmates, and participating in the discussion.

HELOISE: You said there was no metaphors, but I think that the whole thing is a metaphor.

MS. BICKLE: I'd ask them [the group] to explain that.

BOBBY: Explain that.

HELOISE: Well, I don't think that he was really talking literally. I think that has meaning.

BOBBY: I couldn't find anything.

SARAH: Well, I think that [unclear] symbolizes love.

HELOISE: Well, I think that he's saying that his father come in at, came in at night to see if he was, like, sleeping, or whatever. But, like, when the father thinks that he's awake, he doesn't show much love, and so his father coming in at night when he's sleeping peacefully kind of symbolizes his love, to show that he really does love his son.

Although Heloise begins to explain the deeper meaning she sees in the piece, Sarah (who had mentioned symbolism earlier) begins to explore at a more literal level, and others join in. Other class members listen to their ideas, then disagree, telling why.

SARAH: His dad might have a heart problem.

BOBBY: What?

JERRY: And he wants to heal it.

SARAH: He wants to heal it by thinking about the good part. . . .

BOBBY: I just have . . . one of our questions was, do you think that the father cares and loves the child? And did the child care and love the father? That was one of our questions?

MICHELLE: I don't think it's that this father has [unclear] about the heart. It's just a way of showing that somebody cares about him.

HONEY: I agree with her because it just doesn't seem like that kind of home where it's about [unclear] heart, more affection.

HELOISE: Well, I think that the way that they're saying that he would
    like it, not everyone is going to come in and check.
FERN: The father, like, really loved the son.

Michael turns the focus back to deeper meanings conveyed through
words, and the discussion turns back to underlying metaphors and sym-
bols, although these technical words are not necessarily used.

MICHAEL: If someone had a good heart, that means that they're nice.
    They're not, like, I don't think this poem's about, like, what you
    said before, like, they have a heart problem.
SARAH: In the literal sense, secret heart is love for his son, shown
    secretly.
MICHELLE: I think when they say the secret heart, I think it's secret. I
    think when they say heart, they're talking about something like
    something like love inside it that becomes a live sweet thing.

As the discussion continues, Sarah seems to be approaching the piece
less literally. She responds to a question from Stu in a way that reflects
how her treatment of metaphorical language relates to her understanding of this poem.

STU: The question is, why does he think about a glowing heart?
SARAH: Well, I think that the glowing heart, and how the poet made it
    at night, and the heart glowing, could symbolize that it was a
    secret. I mean he says, I don't think that the heart was actually
    glowing. I think the author used it to describe the heart.

TEACHABLE MOMENTS

Although the students did all the teaching during the preceding discussion, the adult teacher often plays an overt role in students' development of literary knowledge. In literary discussions, "teachable" moments
occur, often in response to the students' own comments and queries.
These moments result from intellectual curiosity and the desire to communicate more effectively. The concepts and ways to talk about them
grow from social settings where the desire to communicate and ready-
to-hand interactive support co-occur (Rogoff, 1990; Wertsch, 1991).
Hence, "teaching" is situation-specific, growing from the learners' attempts to make sense and communicate and the teachers' sense of what
they can handle, rather than from a predetermined notion of what technical language or concepts they "should" be learning.

In these situations, teachers make many on-the-spot decisions based on how familiar they think their students are with the literary terms and the concepts underlying them. Four situations in particular occur in classes that provide environments for active thinking and learning:

- Students have neither the concepts nor the language to talk about them.
- Students have the concepts but not the language.
- Students have less complex understandings than their language implies.
- Students have the language and the concepts and are ready to think about them in more sophisticated ways.

Each of these situations is discussed in the following sections, together with the responses that teachers may make.

Neither the Concepts nor the Language

In all classes, there are instances when students introduce ideas that are only beginnings, buds from which tomorrow's understandings will eventually grow. Students begin to raise ideas but do not have the concepts or the words to form them in ways that they can express, reflect on, or share with others. In such instances, teachers can sometimes pick up on the student's idea and provide support for further learning by creating a situation in which the concept is used and flagged. In such situations, because the concept is relatively new, teachers don't expect students to learn the concept or remember what to call it; they merely create the situation as a way to introduce and contextualize the idea. The teacher "flags" the concept, often using a label that might be picked up again later during the same or a subsequent class meeting.

This occurred in Marty's class, prior to the discussion of "The Secret Heart." The students had read several poems and brought up the possibility that some words and phrases might not mean what they ordinarily do. After several students had mentioned this, Marty said, "And that's called a metaphor." Thus she was able to invite her students to consider one aspect of metaphorical language—how it opens new possibilities for interpretation—and through this, they began to build an understanding of the concept.

We can see another example of this no concept–no language situation as Barbara helps her students focus on characterization through a role-playing activity during their reading of "Charles" (1976) by Shirley Jackson (see Chapter 2). Her students had done role playing earlier in the year but did not use this experience to develop a deeper understanding of the character: "It impacted on how they interpreted the story because they kept talking about this person's interpretation, but they didn't realize what they were doing." To help them experience the notion of characterization, Barbara asks the students during a later class meeting to work in small groups to prepare and assume the roles of the characters in particular situations: the parents right after the PTA meeting, the father and Laurie the next morning after breakfast, the mother and teacher at the PTA meeting the night after the story ends, the teacher and Laurie the next day at school, and the mother and Laurie as Laurie leaves for school at the end of the story. The students are to discuss the ways in which they imagine the characters might think and behave.

Barbara explains the activity: "What you're trying to do is talk about what are these characters like, how are they going to behave. And when you get up [and role-play], you put yourself in that role and you become that character and you act the way that character would behave." She plans to engage the students in a written conversation from the characters' perspectives and end with a combined role play and large group discussion, in which the class members will "talk" to the characters and ask them questions, and the role players will respond. Barbara moves from group to group, offering help when needed.

Ms. Furst: All right, now, tell me how this is going to work. How's the mother gonna react when she finds out her son is . . .
Mary: Surprised . . . because this mother seems to see her son as perfect, as an angel.
Ms. Furst: And then what?
James: I'm kind of irresponsible and dumb. . . .
Ms. Furst: (*Supporting them before moving on to another group*) It's important to talk about what kind of people these characters are, and decide how they would behave. How is the teacher gonna treat Laurie? What kind of person is the teacher?

Although the term *characterization* was never used, this lesson helped the students develop understandings underlying the concept.

When discussing similar no concepts–no language situations in her first-grade class, Tanya said:

Well, I think it is very helpful for children to begin to be able to identify and categorize in their minds what they are reading. I can remember in the past doing fairy tales, and then introducing a number of other stories for fun, knowing the stories were not fairy tales, and having us debate, discuss the elements and debate whether we thought they fell into the category. . . . We certainly talk about fiction and nonfiction. . . . I guess the thing is I don't realize how much my children learn in terms of vocabulary because my approach is to use it [build concepts through activities in context]. I just model it rather than say today we are going to learn a new word.

The Concepts, but Not the Language

There are times when students want to communicate certain ideas about the literature they are reading, have some knowledge of the concept they are after, but do not have the literature-specific ways to talk about that concept. They can engage in everyday talk about the general issue, but they can't communicate the more specific concept because they do not have the literary language to do so. In these situations, teachers focus on offering appropriate language for the students to use, not on helping them think about the concept in more complex ways.

For example, in Louise's first-grade class, a student responds to a story by saying, "It makes me giggle." Louise knows that the student had talked about "funny stories" before and therefore has a basic idea about the subgenre. In response to the student's comment, she says, "So, you think it's a humorous story."

In Tanya's class, Jeff struggles for language to express his ideas:

JEFF: Maybe they, just, like, [unclear] where you can't retell it, like you can't use it without [unclear] the book or something.
Ms. WEBER: Okay. Like when there's a copyright.
JEFF: Yeah!

The next example comes from Kendall Mason's 12th-grade class, during a discussion of authenticity in the text of Sophocles' *Antigone*. Students are exploring the issue of whether to accept a controversial passage in one of the versions they have read. At the end of the discussion, Kendall restates the two critical perspectives the students have identified in their own language and then uses the more specific terms *scholarship* and *psychology* to label the competing concepts underlying the students' analyses. Although the students do not use these terms during the lesson, they know that Kendall is providing a restatement of what they have been saying.

REBA: (*Introducing the scholarship issue*) I think that if it was clearly part of the original, if Sophocles had originally intended for it to be in there, then definitely it should be in there, because it's a very important passage. Because it's, like, another whole side of it. But if there is a discrepancy, if you can't be certain that it was part of it, then I don't think it should be because of the difference that it shows.

MR. MASON: That's a very safe decision. If it can be what? Established beyond a doubt that Sophocles intended it to be there, then we have no right to meddle. But if that can't be, you want it out.

ARNEY: I think they should trash it.

MR. MASON: What?

ARNEY: Trash it, get rid of it. (*Introducing the psychological point of view*) Because it contradicts what we've come to see Antigone as, and I don't believe that she has this character that would be so headstrong, and kind of go back on her words and everything at the end.

The students continue to discuss these options for some time, until Kendall recaps the options, suggesting greater definition.

TERRY: I would take it out I think, because I think it lessens the effect of making her a tragic hero, because she winds up dying, but then she says, "Well maybe it wasn't because of this, but it was because of this."

MR. MASON: So, it reduces her, diminishes her character, maybe diminishes, but not cheapens [this idea had been voiced the previous day and again earlier in class]. Does it cheapen her character? Do you want to go that far?

TERRY: Yeah.

DAN: I think it should be left in. But obviously when you print it, have an asterisk and some statement that it's been disputed. . . .

KITTY: I said take it out. . . . It ruins the image that she was like that.

REBA: She was afraid of the consequences of her actions.

MR. MASON: (*Synthesizing the students' comments*) In other words, for reasons Reba says . . . (*writing the words* psychology *and* scholarship *on the board*), so could we focus on that? The two reasons we're disputing here is, that Reba uses, is that scholarship could establish it's there, regardless of what? Of its (*points to word*), psychology, then it stays. But if it's ambiguous, then we can only look to the what (*points to the word*), the psychology. Is inconsistent, as Dave would say. Right?

Less Complex Understandings Than Language Implies

Students often have what Vygotsky (1962) refers to as pseudoconcepts. From other people in their environment, they pick up language that they use before they have come to understand the fuller meanings those labels imply. Pseudoconcepts are a natural and normal part of learning, part of situations that all of us have been in. Often, through using terminology that we only partially understand, we come to a greater understanding of the concepts themselves—we learn through interaction. When using technical terminology in discussing a nagging lower back pain with the doctor, for example, we may go home feeling like "experts" because we have learned more about disk degeneration than we ever knew before. This also occurs in school, when students use literary language but have less complete notions of the underlying concepts than their words imply. In these circumstances, it is easy for a teacher to read too much into what the student says, assuming that because the words were used, the underlying ideas are also fully present. But this is often not the case.

Sometimes, a student's statement is a giveaway, with a word or phrase used inappropriately or clumsily. This is an opportunity for guidance from the teacher, as in this excerpt from Jane Robbins's class:

SAM: The characterization is thin. You know, he isn't in the story a lot.
Ms. ROBBINS: Have you been able to develop a fairly good picture of
    the character? Was there enough material in the story to help you
    form a vision of the character?

Sometimes, however, it is hard to distinguish what students say from what they mean. When in doubt, teachers can ask, "Is this what you mean? Let me see if I understand you." Or they can provide new experiences and elaborations to extend students' understanding of the labels they already know.

Both the Language and the Concepts

In thoughtful literary discussions, there are many instances when students have appropriate language and concepts that can become richer and more complex through further discussion. In these instances, the teacher can use transitional words and ideas as a sort of conceptual bridge from the more general (or less complex) to the more specific (or more sophisticated) to help students contextualize and understand the new.

For example, in Greta's primary-grade class, the language used to refer to certain types of books changes over the course of the school year from "true story" to "nonfiction" to "historical analysis." The language changes as the students' concepts continue to grow, allowing them to differentiate among more types of books. Similarly, in Paula's primary-grade class, there is a transition during the year from focusing solely on the way the students feel in response to a piece to discussing mood, the author's possible purpose in creating that mood, and textual devices that might have suggested the mood to the students.

In Tanya's class, the students hear a number of folktales and legends— adaptations as well as retellings. During each new experience, Tanya identifies the type and invites discussion. Although the students know at a superficial level what the labels refer to, the distinction between adaptation and retelling is unclear, as this exchange illustrates:

JEREMY: Did it say "adapted" or the other one [retold] in front?
    [referring to the title page, where this information is included]
TANYA: It doesn't say "adapted," and that's a very good question. So
    this author didn't do what Terry Colin does. This author says
    "retold." I'm very glad you brought that up, Jeremy, because this
    author said she retold the story, which means that she's telling it
    very close to the real, real original story. Now, Terry Colin
    adapted her stories and that means that she didn't quite make
    them exactly like they've been told.

Here is an example from Kendall Mason's class discussion of *Antigone*. The idea of a tragic flaw was brought up many times by the students, during several class meetings. They worked easily with the classical notion of the concept. Kendall never focused them on the term, but he used it in his responses to their comments about Antigone and whatever flaws they thought she might possess. In the example that follows, Kendall returns to the notion of a tragic flaw in the final lesson of this unit by introducing an essay by Arthur Miller that argues against the existence of such a flaw. Kendall uses Miller's essay and the ensuing discussion to help expand the students' notion of the concept.

MR. MASON: Now, Arthur Miller wrote the essay which you have in
    front of you in response to a long-held theory that a tragic hero,
    to be somebody of great stature, nobly born, whose role in life
    was to be of great significance, the theory implied that common
    people couldn't be tragic at all. Whatever it means to be tragic.
    You read the Aristotle, you know, Aristotle said tragedy is the
    fall of a great man, who by some fault of his own, "flaw," right?
    But, according to Miller, the flaw is not really a flaw, but maybe a
    strength, right? . . . See, what's Hamlet's tragic flaw?
MANY STUDENTS: He hesitates.

MR. MASON: Is it? His hesitation? Can't make a decision? Mario Cuomo, as you know, when he was, or was becoming, or was going to run, wasn't going to run, they called him Hamlet on the Hudson because he couldn't make up his mind. So, Hamlet's indecision is called his tragic flaw. But then there are those in another school who said that his tragic flaw is his very strength, his sensitivity, his unwillingness to kill.

The discussion continues.

The four kinds of learning and teaching interactions I have just described are not age-related, sequential, or unitary. As I have illustrated through classroom examples, at every age, in every grade, and with all human beings, some concepts and language are more familiar and others are less well known; there is always much to be learned. Concepts and the language associated with them change and grow more sophisticated with experience. They grow from quizzical readers' explorations in thought-provoking instructional contexts—in which the focus is on developing ideas and interpretations. Experience is critical; students need a variety of texts and related activities to provide the contexts in which literary knowledge becomes relevant and useful.

Some people think that having literary knowledge is the mark of a "literate" or "educated" person. Others think that knowledge of the vocabulary and underlying concepts enhances both the enjoyment and the understanding of literature. Still others think that this knowledge helps students understand the structure of literary texts and thus enhances their ability to write. Based on my view of literate thinking described in Chapter 1, I think that students' ability to engage in the sorts of discussions illustrated in this chapter is a useful indicator of their literacy. Such participation is often more revealing than a traditional measure of their ability to read, write, or replicate literal meanings or others' ideas. In classes where discussion is thought provoking and texts are inviting, literary knowledge and concepts are used and learned across the grades—and go hand in hand with literate behaviors and literacy development. In such classrooms, literary concepts become an integral part of how the students think about and express ideas. The literary language they learn grows from their involvement in discussions that matter.

Thus, the development of literary language and concepts goes hand in hand with the material read, the focus of the class as a literary discussion community, and the students' desire to participate in that community. In many significant ways, this process of teaching and learning literary knowledge is similar to the process of language (and concept) acquisition of many middle-class Western children described by many researchers (e.g., Brown, 1958; Weir, 1962). Such children learn language through experiences with parents and caregivers who have a good hunch about what the children know and are reaching toward. These caregivers create new environments and capitalize on existing ones, flag new concepts, and help children refine their language and understandings. Although teachers have different life histories (e.g., language, culture, and experiences) from students and can never play the role of "knowing" mother, they need to build bridges, "cross relational waters" (Dyson, 1994), and help students do the same. If, as Delpit (1988) suggests, the language of success and power in Western society needs to be made available to all, the kinds of interaction patterns I have just discussed may help equalize opportunities.

9

Literature Across the Curriculum

Thus far my discussion has focused on literary understanding in English language arts classes. However, in the first chapter of this book, I argued for a new conception of the role of literature education in all schooling, one that views literary understanding as an important aspect of intelligent thought that is useful in everyday life, on the job, and in academic learning across the curriculum. Now I turn to the issue of literature across the curriculum.

It should be no surprise that I think that literature needs to be regarded as more than a type of text or kind of content—rather, as a way to think. If literature is to add another dimension of thought and knowing to students' learning experiences, the purposes for using literature need to be different from the purposes for using textbooks. But this requires a major shift in teachers' thinking about what counts as knowing in their classrooms. Science and social studies teachers, even more so than English teachers, have been schooled in a logic-oriented tradition. Such teachers have sometimes created extensive literature libraries in their classrooms, but they have used them primarily for discursive purposes— as supplementary materials from which students are expected to mine information. For them, enhancing students' understandings of the content through interiorized experience is often a radically new concept.

Unfortunately, the move to develop literature-based instruction across the curriculum has sometimes focused more on appropriate materials than on ways to nurture students' explorations of horizons of possibilities. Although "trade" books add breadth of material to the content classroom, neither their presence nor their use necessarily provides students with alternative ways to enrich their understandings from a literary perspective. Making the shift is not an easy task—even for English teachers who are highly motivated to incorporate such alternatives (see Chapter 6).

Sometimes programs that are specifically designed to integrate literature into the curriculum miss the mark. They "import" literature material into subject classes as a separate offering, keeping it apart from the
usual course work—for separate "supplementary" lessons. These lessons may even be taught by a "visiting" English teacher if the subject
teacher feels uncomfortable working with the literary material or considers it to be the English teacher's area. Sometimes the content area
teacher makes connections between the literature and course content,
sometimes not. In either case, such material often becomes an interesting but separate experience for both teachers and students. These "im-
ported experiences" occur when literature is used *as* the curriculum
instead of *in* the curriculum.

INTRODUCING LITERARY THINKING
IN SUBJECT AREA CLASSROOMS

What roles do the different orientations toward meaning have in various
school subjects? Across subjects as diverse as social studies, history,
civics, general science, biology, physics, and English, horizons-of-
possibilities and point-of-reference thinking interact in productive ways
even in classrooms that have made no special effort to incorporate literature (J. A. Langer, 1995). They provide students with alternative vantage points from which to approach problems and build fuller understandings of the topics they study. Although examples of both kinds of
thinking can be found in all subject areas, they occur in different amounts
and serve different purposes, depending on both the particular subject
and how it is taught. Point-of-reference thinking naturally predominates
in all but the English courses. However, even in other subject areas,
teachers sometimes invite horizons-of-possibilities thinking—and students use it—as a way to enrich understanding.

Creating Scenarios

Literary thinking occurs in several different ways in content area classes.
One way is through the use of story: When a lesson involves seemingly
remote technical principles or systems, teachers may make connections
to students' everyday lives by creating a scenario in which they are
involved.

In the following example, Teresa Breen's high school biology class
is studying the reproductive system. She knows that her students are
interested in the general topic, but she wants them to understand both

the terminology and the biological mechanisms. She also wants them to feel comfortable talking openly about the topic and raising questions. To accomplish this, she uses various story forms, often inviting the students into a collective envisionment-building interaction. In the example here, she orchestrates the development of a communal dialogue, placing herself in the role of naive stranger and the students as informants. A play of fact and fantasy ensues.

Ms. BREEN: I have gonads? I thought only boys had gonads.
CLASS: You have ovaries.
Ms. BREEN: Oh, I have ovaries and Gene's got ovaries?
GENE: No I don't.
TINA AND OTHERS: No, he's got testes, at least we hope so.
Ms. BREEN: But, should I use the same name for both?
JOHN: You can if you want to, but you can also say testes and ovaries.
OTHER STUDENTS: Yeah, yes. Right.
MARY: Yeah, it's more specific, so people will know just what sex you
    mean.

At other times, Teresa tells a story and invites the students to create a scenario.

Ms. BREEN: Sperm and egg, presto-chango, that was me. That egg
    mitosed and you have wonderful me. Let's close our eyes and
    listen to my story, my beginning. Then imagine this as your
    beginning. We all have cells that will grow into sperms or eggs.
    So, I'm at the end of my mother's uterus, okay, and my ovaries
    are forming. Right then, I have all the eggs I will have for the rest
    of my life. That's it. If I didn't get any eggs then . . .

She then steps out of the story, to add an aside that invites them to connect their scenarios to their understanding of reproduction, their point-of-reference topic.

Ms. BREEN: Men can always go on and make more and more and
    more [sperm]. It's a little different process, but every time you
    make a sperm or egg, you cut the original cell in half.

In turn, the students create envisionments of the new life and use this as a place from which to return to their primary point-of-reference orientation and begin asking point-of-reference questions about reproduction. For instance:

JOHN: Wait a minute, so you have forty-six right now?
Ms. BREEN: Right. Then, when I make an egg, it gets cut in half. That's when an egg ripens, for you are making sperm all the time.

The primary orientation throughout the lesson is point of reference; the goal of understanding the reproductive system is never out of sight. But within this context, literary thinking becomes a useful alternative approach that extends and enriches the pool of knowledge and experience the students can call upon. They step in and out of their created story-world several times throughout the lesson. For instance, when Teresa turns later to talking about menopause and late-in-life pregnancies, she recalls the scenario created earlier in order to contextualize and personalize the discussion.

Ms. BREEN: Remember, my eggs are there since I'm conceived. I'm forty-two, but my eggs are almost a year older. Imagine how long, a chance for defects.

The students use the stories of their own lives later on as well, again providing a more familiar framework within which to contextualize their questions and analyses. For instance:

PAUL: I got my forty-six chromosomes from my mom and dad, from the egg and sperm, twenty-three and twenty-three, but why do I look more like my father?

Thus the creation of a scenario is a device for providing an interiorized dimension to the students' developing understandings. It provides an alternative route to constructing their overall meanings—an alternative but complementary route to understanding.

Opening Up the Topic

Another way that teachers use horizons-of-possibilities thinking is as motivation, before the students are to get down to work. Although story-making forms such as the ones just illustrated are sometimes used, this is not always the case. Sometimes the focus is on the students' treatment of the overall whole and the changing horizon. As discussed in Chapter 3, one of the major differences between the two orientations (maintaining a point of reference and exploring horizons of possibilities) is in the way people treat the developing whole. Point-of-reference thinking creates a fixed topic or hypothesis to focus thinking (before going on to another topic or hypothesis), whereas horizons-of-possibilities thinking offers an open door to constant construal and reconstrual of the whole. In exploring horizons of possibilities, students may be invited to step into a more personal "story-making" episode, as in Teresa's class, or to explore the topic as a whole in a more open-ended way, with the point of reference temporarily removed. Both are aspects of literary understanding; both involve exploring horizons of possibility, but they involve slightly different foci and serve slightly different ends in content area classes. One involves a shift in what to think about, from information building to story or scenario making; the other stays closer to the topic but opens up what can be thought about to include the topic itself.

Students are given room to explore horizons before beginning to study a new topic when teachers ask such questions as What would you think if . . . ? Thus Stella Ryan began her high school science class by asking, "Have you ever seen a rotten apple? Tell us about it." As the students begin to respond, she does not merely evoke prior knowledge about fermentation but encourages the students to tell stories about their rotten-apple experiences. Later, Stella helps them associate the sights and smells they have recounted with the process of fermentation, which they are beginning to study.

Encouraging students to draw on all aspects of their previous experience and knowledge to create literary worlds can add a complementary dimension to their developing understandings. At times, they may engage in such storylike thinking as, "This reminds me of a time when. . . ." At other times, the ability to explore ideas without the fixedness of a point of reference may open them to thoughts that they might not otherwise have considered.

Particularizing the Abstract

Students use horizons-of-possibilities thinking in all their classes even when this is not explicitly invited by their teachers, and they do so in productive ways. They often explore possibilities when they consider alternative explanations and interpretations, when they go about trying to solve a problem, or when they are simply stuck and spin scenarios in an attempt to move on. Consider the following example, in which a group of high school students is discussing the problems and effects of certain types of government expenditures and the difficult decisions a president must make about them. Rather than dealing with the issues in the abstract, they use a present-day scenario to consider What if . . . ?

CLAUDE: Wait, there's one thing we haven't talked about. Are we
    better off without all the social welfare programs?
ROSE: The deficit would probably be even worse.
TOM: Right.
ROSE: Our deficit would be even more without it.
CLAUDE: If they say the deficit is like a major problem, then they are
    already saying that we have to cut social programs.
TOM: Right. I mean, what else was he gonna do?
CLAUDE: Cut the military programs?
ROSE: Right. But then we would be in the middle of the cold war still.

In this case, the students created a sketchy scenario from which to spin
possibilities. Such scenarios are often woven together as group members share their experiences, as in the following example from another
group of students studying Coelenterata.

PHYLMA: (*Looking at jars of jellyfish, hydra, and sea anemones*) They're
    cute, they're sexy, but I think they sting.
CARA: Yeah, I think they sting too. They remind me of when we went
    to Florida to see my grandmother and at the beach things were
    all washed on shore and there were signs to be careful of stings.
JACK: I was in Seaworld and they had a tidal pool where you could
    stick your hand in the water, and I pet an anemone. I thought I
    might get stung, but the person [Seaworld employee] . . . said
    don't worry about it, they can't get through human skin. But I
    was still worried I'd get hurt, but I didn't.
CARA: Maybe the larger ones can. Were those as big as these? Let's
    see if size has anything to do with their danger.
PHYLMA: Maybe they're not each as dangerous even if they're part of
    the same phylum and all have tentacles.

Students create such momentary scenarios to explore horizons of possibilities when "problem solving" with one another. However, if this
kind of thinking is not recognized as important, its potential may be
brushed aside or ignored even when it comes to the teacher's attention.

It is not just that there is a role for literature and for storytelling in enriching instruction within other disciplines; it is that the processes involved in exploring horizons of possibilities can be helpful as students
work through their understandings, even in contexts where the primary
focus is point-of-reference learning. Both orientations can be used as tools
of instruction to help students think more richly and deeply about their
subject.

INTEGRATING LITERATURE ACROSS THE CURRICULUM:
A TEAM APPROACH

Barbara Furst, whose class we visited in earlier chapters, has also been involved in an integrated curriculum effort. This effort offers a good example of literature *in* the curriculum. In Barbara's middle school, the social studies, science, math, and English teachers worked together as a team, with one period daily devoted to project team meetings. Barbara and her colleagues used this time to keep one another apprised of what they were teaching, to discuss students' progress, to coordinate lessons that they would connect but teach separately, and to plan joint lessons and projects. For them, integration meant making links among activities both within and across disciplines. Together, the teachers looked at and discussed the students' journal entries, reflecting on students' writing, thinking, and learning from their individual as well as collective perspectives. They read students' questions with as much care as their comments, treating the questions as evidence of the kinds of issues the students were concerned about and grappling with. In turn, the students' comments (oral as well as written) were used as input for the teachers' planning about what to teach next and how to coordinate across subjects.

Because integrating literature across the curriculum was a new effort, the teachers met in small groups to discuss the reading of literature as part of their courses. At one point, for example, each teacher chose a biography in his or her subject area to read and then discuss with colleagues. Together, they reflected on their engagement in the activity and on the ways in which their "book talk" had increased their own understanding. They also used their experiences with the biographies to discuss instructional approaches. During these meetings, they focused on how they listened to and questioned one another, what had spurred them to consider new ideas, and how similar approaches to thinking could be supported in their own classrooms. In team meetings at the beginning of the year, Barbara discussed her own attempts to develop an envisionment-building classroom and modeled some of the activities that worked for her.

The project team focused on developing a common understanding of ways in which the students thought and learned with the use of literature. They were not concerned with how to import language arts into their course content, but with how literature could help students learn their particular course content more fully. The teachers preferred to maintain the disciplinary integrity of their courses but wanted to provide more well-rounded support for students' thinking and learning.

However, coteaching was not uncommon. Barbara and Boyd Washington (a social studies teacher), for example, opened the walls between their classrooms for a joint unit on early American history, literature, and life. Their students saw a movie, *The Bridge of Adam Rush*, which depicted Pennsylvania at the turn of the 19th century through the eyes and experiences of a child. The boy, who grew up in cosmopolitan Philadelphia until his father died, must return to his family in rural Pennsylvania. On his journey to the farm, he has flashbacks of his elegant city life, all set up in contrast to the rough and hardworking farm experiences his new life brings. He grows up and grows "wiser" as he helps his stepfather build a bridge.

Boyd tied this movie to his unit on early U. S. history, the period after independence and before the Civil War. Barbara tied the film to her unit on historical fiction. Both used it to stimulate the students to explore the characters' lives and to view them from personal, historical, cultural, and economic perspectives. They also provided opportunities for the students to focus on ways in which history works its way into historical fiction, and what that means for readers.

The team members fostered integration in other ways too. Ethan Jones's science class collected and read scientific articles about the topics they were studying. This coincided with a unit in Barbara's class on science fiction. The teachers brought the two together by asking the students to consider how the science articles they had read for Ethan's class could be used to contribute to a science fiction story, one that was factually correct in its inception yet explored horizons of possibilities in ways that could capture the imaginations of readers of fiction. This activity drew directly on both point-of-reference and horizons-of-possibility thinking—from the vantage point of reading, writing, and discussion as well as across disciplines.

Another time, teachers from each of the subject areas (English, mathematics, social studies, and science) worked cooperatively on a unit using a videodisc as well as firsthand experiences—following a fictional family on an expedition that involved them in using knowledge from each subject area. The students wrote from the perspectives of the characters as well as from their own perspectives, and they solved problems and explored needed information from both orientations, as relevant to the particular activity. The videodisc became the impetus, activity, and initial data source for the integrated project. All collaborating teachers read and responded to the students' journals, and the teachers kept journals as well, as part of their ongoing thinking and communicating.

As this school's experiences illustrate, integration of literature into the curriculum need not mean that all lessons are cotaught throughout the year, nor even on a regular basis. In the case of Barbara's team, none of the teachers in any subject area ever felt that they had stepped away from their own fields or were teaching something they were unprepared to teach. They team-taught or cotaught when it seemed useful, when it could add more to their students' learning than if they had worked alone. Their professional collaboration often prompted them to rethink the themes, the essential overall issues, that provided the critical connections between course content and personal understandings (e.g., Applebee, 1994; Walmsley, 1994). To this group of teachers, this seemed to be a sensible approach to collaboration and integration. It valued their differences in expertise, stimulated them as professionals, and provided room for them to make and shift plans based on their best professional judgments about their students' needs and the particular demands of their own subject areas. This approach also provided room for the flexibility and inventiveness needed to spark the best in teachers and students.

LITERATURE AND WRITING

Although no chapter on literature across the curriculum would be complete without mentioning the uses of writing, I find this a difficult thing to do—not because writing has no place in the envisionment-building classroom, but rather because it is so pervasive that it becomes part of the seamless web of language and thought.

I have always been a proponent of the integration of writing across the curriculum, but I have often been uncomfortable with the ways in which this goal has been carried out. More often than not, integration has meant various sorts of turn taking between reading and writing rather than a true integration of the two in the service of some larger meaningful goal. For example, the instructional materials in most currently available reading texts focus on reading comprehension followed by writing activities. Sometimes a prereading writing activity is also presented, and sometimes instruction in the writing process is offered. Although these formats involve students in more writing activities than may have been the case in previous editions of current texts, the acts of reading and writing are still separated in time and purpose. Writing is rarely used as an integral part of sense making, and reading is rarely used as an act of sense sharing. English and reading and language arts lessons across the grades often show a similar serialization of reading and writing, even when textbooks are not used.

However, in an envisionment-building classroom, these separations disappear—from the minds of the teachers, the experiences of the students, and the activities and interactions that constitute the lessons. When students' thinking is the center of concern, reading and writing are never regarded as skills, activities, or ends in themselves but as tools of language that are available to be used to enhance the development of students' envisionments. The pragmatic goal of stimulating thinking creates a natural integration of reading, writing, and speaking.

In envisionment-building classrooms, reading and writing are entwined throughout the lessons as students bring sense and make sense. Reading, writing, and discussion interplay as students move among personal (or more solitary) and public (or more shared) worlds, as well as among less formal and more formal expressions of language and thought. These interrelated activities provide students with an array of opportunities to generate, review, extend, reflect on, and sharpen their understandings and interpretations. Students read, write, and talk about literature as well as read, write, and create their own.

The envisionment-building classroom is likely to include a great variety of different writing activities: freewriting, quick-writing, brainstorming, journal entries, reading logs, oral readings, role playing, written and oral conversations, small group and whole class presentations, portfolios, artwork, essays, computer graphics, and the like. Any given type of writing activity, however, can serve a variety of purposes, and an understanding of its role in students' thinking requires an understanding of its pragmatic intent—for the student as well as the teacher.

Marty Bickle uses an array of writing activities to invite her students to collect their thoughts and reflect on their envisionments. She believes that this provides a way for students to "pull their thoughts together" in preparation for moving beyond, to involve students who tend to be quiet, and to "keep track of their ideas as they change." She commented on her writing activities:

> I use questions about the story a lot. I ask them to tell what they remember from the day before and where their thinking is at the beginning and end of a piece. We use it to reflect on how their thinking has changed. I use sequels as a way of expanding thinking. . . . I've had the kids write dialogues between different characters from two different stories. You know, what would happen if these two people met? A lot of their writing instruction is also literature based [using the literature as models]. Writing can often be more reflective than discussion, and the activities can complement one another. Writing lets them develop their own thoughts . . . and they come back to discussion with richer ideas.

In Marty's class, reading, writing, and discussion act cooperatively to extend students' thinking. Each writing task has its own purpose, and the kind of writing her students do is affected by that purpose. As Tanya said, "When the students write, they know they do something with that writing." Sometimes it is for them to reflect on; other times to share and build on; and sometimes it is an exhibition piece to show to others.

Thus writing provides a record of different moments in the envisionment-building process. It provides a way for the thoughtful student to freeze ideas in time, to pull together a present understanding from which to move on. Thus reading, writing, and discussing work together, as vehicles for sharing and reflection—for growth in the varieties of awareness that literature calls forth.

10

Closing Thoughts: Literature in School and Life

I cannot end this book without a discussion of a central issue I raised in Chapter 1: that of the contribution of literary understanding to personal, social, and intellectual development. In one sense, these topics highlight the outcomes of literary studies, but in another, they need to be seen in a new light. The last decade of the 20th century heralded a period of intense debate about issues of marginalization and power—debates taking place not only in the halls of academia but throughout society and around the world. It was an era when the unthinkable became reality. Marginalized voices became powerful, and past powers evaporated. In 1984, who could have imagined that Nelson Mandela, after spending 27 years in Pollsmoor and Victor Verster prisons, would at the age of 75 be elected the first president of a united South Africa ruled by a black majority sharing power with a white minority? Who could have imagined the disintegration of the Soviet Union and the ensuing wars for power among marginalized peoples that the world forgot it had forgotten? We can never again deny that radical voices demanding transformations breathe the possible and must be heard. The horizons of possibility that we explore today can help shape the actualities of tomorrow.

The exploration of possibilities and the examination of multiple perspectives offer ways to achieve greater equality among voices, particularly those that have been marginalized. The act of exploring horizons takes the unfamiliar or unexamined and renders it particular, personal, imaginable. In envisionment-building classrooms, teachers and students do not expect to be of one voice. In fact, they come to expect and welcome differences, assuming that their own and others' understandings will develop through the dialogue that ensues. They also assume that although dialogue fosters a sense of shared community, it leads neither to homogenization nor to consensus.

The ability to participate fully in the conversation is critical; consensus silences marginalized voices (Barbules & Rice, 1991), whereas open horizons invite inquiry and expect difference. When all can participate fully, the group changes. Power and control shift as individuals' thinking develops, and social expectations and relationships also change. Envisioning literature classrooms and the pedagogical principles that underlie them provide a context where inquiry and communication are open and where changes in views, perspectives, and roles are expected (Bereiter, 1994; Philips, 1994).

Schools remain sites where cultural conflicts must be confronted. The cultural histories, achievements, languages, and entitlements of all students—of humankind—can be addressed in ongoing and essential ways. The end goals of education are not only academic but also social and personal. Schools can contribute to the development of human beings who use imagination to gain insight and vision, sensitivity and strategy—who can conceive of ways to change not only themselves but also the world.

Schools need to embody an expanded view of community, one that is based not on conformity but on plurality, grounded in difference. As members of an increasingly multicultural community, Maxine Greene (1993) argues, we need to find significance in hearing multiple voices that have been silenced over the years, enriching the ongoing conversation, opening experience as well as possibility. This involves "a regard for distinctiveness as well as reaching toward connectedness . . . for imaginative efforts to cross the distances to look through diverse others' eyes" (p. 16). Greene calls for openness and variety as well as inclusion and individualization, an avoidance of fixedness and stereotypes. Although cultural heritages create differences that must be honored, individuals are deeply affected by a variety of experiences in their lives. We need to avoid masking their personal histories in our stereotypes about cultural differences. Greene suggests the need to open spaces for students to tell their stories: "Learning to look through multiple perspectives, young people may be helped to build bridges among themselves, they may be provoked to heal and transform" (p. 17).

A focus on literature as a way of thinking provides an opportunity to consider how schools can make such transformations thinkable. My primary argument centers on the act of literary understanding as a way to know, on providing a way to conceptualize how that kind of thought develops and suggesting ways to teach it. In a sense, this is a political argument. There is always something another person knows, has experienced, and "reads" into a situation that is unknown to others. This notion underlies Bakhtin's (1981) concepts of dialogue and intertextuality. Validation of and respect for difference preclude the existence of a single unchallenged perspective. The envisionment-building classroom expects to hear all voices because hearing others' construals is a way to extend and move one's own thinking forward. This does not mean that conflicts are neutralized, nor that resistance is eradicated. Instead, students have an opportunity to participate in a community where they can express their thoughts and read "against" texts—where they can develop their ideas and have an audience to respond to them.

Through literature, students can become aware of how their ways of reading are complicated and implicated by their personal and group histories. In a sense, envisionment-building classrooms can be thought of as the "safe houses" that Mary Louise Pratt (1991) describes in her paper on contact zones (see also Bizzell, 1994). Contact zones are the inevitable battlefields on which individuals play out their group histories and asymmetrical relationships. Here the interactions between text and student (student and student, institution and student) reflect their different cultural and political histories, and the stakes can be high. Although working in contact zones is critical, Pratt believes that students also need "safe houses"—social and intellectual contexts where people can constitute themselves as communities based on trust and shared understanding. Safe houses are places that offer "temporary protection from the legacies of oppression, [and that allow students to develop] claims on the world that they can then bring into the contact zone" (Pratt, 1991, p. 40). The envisionment-building classroom can certainly be a contact zone, but it can be a safe house as well.

I hope that the classrooms I have described and the theory that underlies them will provide a pedagogical frame to help students and teachers use what they know better and more effectively—to voice their own ideas, to hear others in ways that push their own thinking, to be sensitive to viewpoints not necessarily their own, to think deeply and communicate clearly. I also hope that such an approach will give them power—power of voice, control of their growing ideas, and the sense of self that comes from participating in a group of peers who do not always share the same insights or interpretations but who respect one another enough to gain richness from diversity. I hope that it will support a sense of humanity, an expectation that through the differences among people and ideas we will learn not only to better understand the world and how it works but also how to become our best selves.

Inherent in the act of literary understanding is the promise of touching the many-sidedness of human sensibility. It is through the envisionments we develop as we explore new horizons of possibility that we can at least begin to imagine the perspectives of others—in other circumstances, eras, cultures—and be moved to make new sense of ourselves, our times, and our world.

Literature makes us better thinkers. It moves us to see the multi-sidedness of situations and therefore expands the breadth of our own visions, moving us toward dreams and solutions we might not otherwise have imagined. It affects how we go about learning in academic situations, how we solve problems at work and at home. And it moves us to consider our interconnectedness with others and the intrinsic pluralism of meaning; it helps us become more human.

Afterword: Reflections of Teachers and Students

I thought that the readers of this book, having been brought into the lives and thinking of a number of teachers and students, might be curious about their comments after having spent some time envisioning litera-ture—insiders' reflections over time, offered in their own words. The comments were collected in different ways. The teachers who worked with me designing envisionment-building classrooms kept journals, and each December and May they did some reflective freewriting. Some of their jottings follow. We received a couple of letters from students, recalling their experiences in envisionment-building classrooms; one was an English class project and the other a letter from college. Both are here for you to read. We interviewed 33 students who had been in envisionment-building classrooms 2 to 5 years earlier, as well as their current teachers. Some of their comments are included.

The selection process—which comments to include and which to set aside—was difficult for me. There were no negative reviews from any teachers or students, probably because they were active colleagues, shar-ing problems and experimenting with new ways throughout the project. But their recollections differed, and in the end I selected a variety of voices. I hope that their comments provide a sense of what it actually means to experience an envisioning-building classroom.

SOME TEACHERS

First, here are some journal entries and end-of-year notes from some of the teachers.

Sandy Bano

. . . I had taken my teaching of literature for granted and assumed the "old way." Now I see that focusing on student thinking and therefore allowing the student to become familiar (comfortable) with a piece . . . for example using response journals has enhanced classroom discussions because the students . . . aren't "put on the spot" by having to answer a question. Also, after students write in their journals, they've often discussed the work in pairs. Then, by the time we discuss it in a whole classroom situation, the students are usually very comfortable with the topic at hand and discuss freely.

I have been surprised by how trusting they've become of me and each other. I guess because I've said it enough times, they *have come* to believe that everyone's opinion counts, and we should say whatever ideas come to mind. . . . They also learned to deal with someone else disagreeing with their point and have become better at trying to back up their ideas (or question them).

The class has also learned that I won't give or necessarily even know the "right" answer. It was hard for me at the beginning of the school year not to answer a question because I was uncomfortable with the silence. I have gotten much better with that and it happens less frequently because the students know it has to come from them.

One other plus is that I'm constantly evaluating myself. I have learned not to automatically teach the old way. . . . For instance I sometimes don't put enough of myself into the discussions and therefore the scaffolding isn't there. I seem to get so hung up on being "student oriented" that I forget I can be the leader or the director of the discussion without really interfering [with the ideas they are creating].

Loren Verplank

"What does the poem mean to you, Hoss? What are your under-standings of the book so far, Anna? Do you like this story? Why?" Questions. Questions with answers that don't belong to me, the teacher.

Learning how to pose such questions has been a part of the outcome of . . . this year. I'm improving at my ability to ask questions that are truly open-ended during book conferences, allowing for a student to bring his own envisionment of a piece to the discussion.

As much as learning which kinds of questions to ask, I've begun to listen to the responses to such questions. Since the answer belongs to the student, I don't have to compare my expected response with what the child has to say. I can direct all my attention to the student's ideas. In this way, I can try to ask further questions which will encourage each to think more deeply about their understandings.

There is no air of deceptive simplicity to this process of scaffolding. No lesson plans. The child leads the way.

Another insight I've gained is the advantage of talking and thinking in a group. . . . My small band of seventh-grade remedial readers became adept at functioning as a group searching for meaning. By the year's end, they requested me to say nothing during one tape recording; they were secure in how to go about such discussion and wished to show a new member the ropes.

Observing the way these children worked to construct meaning from their reading has forced me to reconsider the very terms *remedial* and *literate*. Are these students so very different from others? Can they be enriched by reading and discussing literature which considers the more complex aspects of the human condition?

Marty Bickle

They walked right into the room in September with a propensity for carrying on long-running jokes and a willingness to try anything. I watched them take risk after risk—sharing personal views on literature, admitting confusion with certain pieces, disagreeing with classmates, defending unpopular positions. In general, they were willing to try.

They told me straight out early in the year they thought they learned more from class discussions and listening to each other than they learned from me. Probably the most valuable thing they learned was to value the ideas of each other while recognizing they were still free to disagree.

Another thing that struck me about the group was their ability to make connections between pieces of literature. For example, they read *The Diary of Anne Frank* early in the year. In the spring they read a poem called "Identity"—initial responses to that poem by kids were everything from confusion to "It's just like me," to "This made me think of Anne Frank."

In a way, I think some of the literature we read stayed in a state of flux for them—shaped in their minds when it was read, reshaped (sometimes) by class discussion and again as they read other pieces and still other voices.

I thought their responses were impressive. They talked about the need for freedom, the importance of being loved, the difficulty making choices, and a lot more—and how the treatment of these ideas was the same or different in the different pieces of literature. . . . I thought their ability to make these kinds of connections and to deal with ideas somewhat abstract was pretty amazing.

I know this sounds a bit like it grew out of one or two pieces of literature. It didn't. It really grew out of a year's worth of work of thinking, rethinking, and sharing.

I think that one of the things that contributed to this was the fact that we never truly got to a sense of closure. Every piece of litera-ture we left was left with some open questions. Since we left things open, it was easy to go back to them. We never went for consensus or right answers. These kids moved up and down through stances. We weren't really following a path as much as we were wandering about.

Tom Borg

For me, the concept of envisionment better articulated my own personal sense of literary comprehension and understanding. It also spoke to where I wanted to take my students when we did pieces of literature in class. For a number of years I had done a poem by Robert Frost titled "The Last Words of Bluebeard as Told to a Child." I had always shared this poem and tried to bring the students into seeing *my* understanding, comprehension, *envisionment* of this work. Now I begin to understand why they did not totally "buy" my ideas. Theirs, of course, were different. But in my "traditional class," there was no room for their ideas nor any sense that ideas, or envisionments, can change over time.

Mine did! That year, shortly after I had done this poem with perhaps two of my classes for the day, one student in our discussion of the poem and what they saw in the piece said something that triggered a significant change in my hard and fast comprehension of the poem.

Two things are significant here. The least of which is that my personal understanding-envisionment had changed. That alone had been sweet for me. But more importantly, this event would not have taken place if we had not been sharing in class our own changing envisionments of the poem. I am now richer, and I hope my students are also.

Cyrus Ford

I have come to realize more and more that an *authority* on any particular interpretation is after all just *one* in a number and not the only or final way of seeing. The notion of having a preconceived plan from which a teacher should not vary comes more and more when I have this notion in my head. It doesn't let me hear what the students may offer, particularly if it is at odds with the plan.

I am an authority (but not the only one) and my views may be as valid or false or changing as anyone's. Interpretation may be as much a revision of beliefs as trying to defend my belief. [It calls for] questioning in such a way as to "move" from center.

Barbara Furst

I have learned to *listen* to my students and to trust their instincts. Throughout the year they have continually proven that their sense of what is important in a piece is right. . . . I have also learned to respect their knowledge and intelligence. Twelve-year-olds are capable of very sophisticated thinking. Their insights have led me to view questions in a different way, directing me to new interpretations.

As the class participates in a discussion of literature, I see changes in the way the class operates. The students have learned to *listen* to one another. I think of Dick at the beginning of the year. New to the school, he quickly became the target of pranks and taunts. Labeled "dumb" early in the year, he struggled to find a place for himself within the class structure. . . . But as he began to trust the give and take of the classroom, he began to offer ideas. The students saw that he was thinking and his status improved. Ken, who remains a disruptive factor, still has important thoughts to contribute, and the students are willing to talk about his ideas even though they are annoyed by his behavior at other times. Dorothy may start her response with, "I disagree with Ruth." Ruth will smile, listen, and respond to Dorothy's concerns in a thoughtful manner.

The students see each other as thinkers, understand that agreement is not required, and delight at looking at many sides of an issue. Students who are Honor Society candidates argue with students in remedial reading. Their academic status dissolves when they are caught up in the thinking and understanding of a story.

Tanya Weber

I realized I needed to train my ear to what the children were saying. First I needed to become more comfortable with the final envisionment questions. I was awkward with it at first and I saw that the children were not used to what I was asking either. Gradually, however, as with other experiences, once they were familiar with this format and felt comfortable sharing responses, I have become more relaxed and able to sit back knowing the children would happily "take the ball" and get the discussion going. I began to see a level of empowerment grow among the children—very subtly at first, but as weeks passed and we had more new comments, and I was able to "up the ante" I began to hear new information from the class. It was then I really knew my ears had become tuned to a higher level too. I needed to listen for new comments that went above and beyond the familiar. Then I had to stop and steer their discussion, not worrying about everyone contributing, but looking forward to the fact that steering in a new direction might actually open up more children and engage them.

One fascinating thing that I found was that some extremely capable children kept themselves in their very safe spot of predicting and connecting. But with the awareness that [exploring horizons of possibilities] was exciting, other children who I may not have expected to hear from some months before, became very involved not just in reacting to others but very much in initiating significant envisionments. . . . The class had reached a point where individuals rethink their own ideas or initial envisionments and will now say, "I don't think that any more. I agree with so and so instead." Another thrill for these first graders was the power to disagree! This whole empowerment issue has overflowed into nonfiction.

SOME STUDENTS, SOME YEARS LATER

Sandi wrote a paper for 10th-grade English, 3 years after her experiences in an envisionment-building classroom. These are her recollections as recounted in that writing assignment.

A smile is a wonderful thing to bestow upon someone, an art which was perfected by my seventh grade English teacher. She possessed a passion for teaching that would shine through in everything she did. Essentially, she had the quality that made students work harder and better than they ever thought possible, just to see her shining face beam toward you like a ray full of sunshine and hope.

Short, but stately, she seemed a throwback from the age of royalty with the curly hair to match. She was always prepared for any situation and always found the time to sit and listen. One of her favorite ways to help other students understand a book was to have a class discussion. In a circle, we, her students, would speak about any aspect of the story we were presently reading. Consequently, another student would agree or disagree, thereby forcing the original speaker to defend and/or rethink his/her statement. Many arguments were started and resolved during her 45-minute period. No one ever felt self-conscious or was afraid to speak out to their classmates because of her calming presence.

Claudia, now in college, wrote a letter about her 11th-grade experiences:

My recollection . . . is that of *a lot* of in-class reading, writing, and responding to different types of literature. The class did a lot of reading, both assigned pieces and books of personal choice. In-class discussion and written response were important aspects of the class and learning environment. The discussion as well as personal journals were emphasized as necessary for further exploring ideas in literature.

I'm not sure that this [class] changed so much as enhanced my thinking of literature. Specific questions that were topics of response helped me to further my understanding of literary works. Instead of seeing works through my eyes alone, the [class] helped me to look at different works through different points of view. Looking at literature from different points of view helps me to look further into different pieces and see meaning that I may not have seen through my initial response to a piece.

The [class] also has helped me to respond immediately to what I read, sometimes by writing my responses down, but also just in terms of personal thinking and reflection. The ability to do this helps me to see beyond my initial reaction; to see something deeper in a piece, perhaps a hidden meaning that the author does not want to be too apparent initially. In college, this helps me to pursue my studies by looking at assignments and literature from different aspects. Especially in college, there are many different ways to approach an assignment or particular piece of literature. The ability to look at such things from different perspectives allows further understanding and an enhanced ability to approach different situations.

Years later, students who have participated in envisionment-building classes remember reading and being read to, writing and talking about books, and asking questions. Most memorable are the discussions and the variety of viewpoints expressed. They also remember the group work and projects. Many students speak about particular works they read, what was discussed, and, in the process of recollection, they often reenter their conversations.

For example, Jason's eyes lit up when he started to talk about *Greyling*. Two years after the experience, he went on to reconstrue his earlier interpretation of the story:

> *Greyling*. I was just thinking about it. Well when the Selchie goes into the water, since humans can't hold their breath, it will turn into a seal. When it's on land it will turn into a human. I thought [2 years ago] maybe it was a costume. It's really a seal that can be transformed into a human. [If I didn't have a chance to talk about it again] for my whole life I would still have it hanging.

Jeff, recollecting his first-grade experience, said:

Discussion [was] sort of fun. . . . Like talking and telling about the parts again, everybody [discussing] made me think of another, sort of made me think of the story in a different point of view. 'Cause they made me think of ideas that you wouldn't have thought before.

Alex, now in fourth grade, also recalls his first-grade class:

We would share our opinions, what parts we liked, what other people were feeling, how was their understanding of the story. A lot of times when people think of ideas it triggers other ideas. Every time somebody says something, it makes discussion longer and more exciting. Yeah, there's more ideas to think about. People go from one idea to another. It's fun to think about what's happening in a story. You can like picture everything at once. It kind of all flows together and changes.

Emil, presently an eighth grader, remembered:

Last year was the first English class where I was required to think on my own. When I think about the class, several things stand out in my memory: lengthy discussions, the poetry unit, and our helpful group projects. The discussions were interesting and many viewpoints were discussed. They helped me not be afraid to state my opinion. I now know that there are no right or wrong answers when literature is being discussed.

Kate, presently in 11th grade, looked 4 years into her past:

It was quite surprising to receive this questionnaire this morning, but scarcely an hour had passed before a flood of memories had surfaced. Mrs. Furst broke the class down into pairs and gave each pair a short story. I don't remember the title, but the one to which my partner and I were assigned dealt with the relationship between two children of different races. Maybe the content of that story has remained with me for so long because my partner and I could have assumed the characters' roles. Neither of us really expected to have anything in common. We were given a tape recorder, and were asked to read the story aloud, injecting our own thoughts and ideas, and questions whenever they arose. . . . Sometimes we were asked to respond in writing as we read, in place of the tape recorder. Discussion usually followed. I remember realizing the varying ways in which literature could be interpreted.

. . . I think that was perhaps the first time that I had been encouraged to think about what I read on a more interpretative basis. We were asked to consider so much more than the literal meaning. I am extremely grateful for having had the opportunity to respond with ideas and questions at any point in reading—it seems that it had a tremendous effect on my comprehension of what I read that year, as it does now. I still keep my journal with me when I read, to take notes of whatever catches my attention. I really love the method of jotting down a few words . . . because it seems that, in reflecting on these spontaneous reactions, whatever it is that I am reading makes so much more sense . . . initial reactions are only pieces and clues.

Mike, a fourth-grader, also made connections between his experiences in an envisionment-building class and his present reading habits:

Sometimes when I'm reading, I take a minute and close the book and think about what has happened. With a real good book I want to savor everything at once. Feeling sometimes when it really makes me feel sad, happy, jumpy, I go back and try to remember how they described the feelings in the book. So I can just go back and read that over in my head to get those feelings over. . . . Sometimes I can relate the book to some things that happened in my life. Sometimes when I'm reading a book it just triggers memories. . . .

As I think more about the book, more ideas start to flow into my mind and I get a different point of view from the book. When I'm reading a real good book, when I'm finishing it, I kind of stare at the cover and think, "Wow, what a great book that was," and I kind of take a breath.

. . . It [the class] taught me to try to look back and understand what's happening, like to make a movie in my head.

Kathy, Rory, Thomas, and John, 2 years later, reflected on their first-grade experiences and made connections to their present habits:

She said, "Close your eyes and imagine a picture, what this girl would look like if she had sparks in her face." Sometimes we would give a prediction. Sometimes we whispered to each other what you could really imagine. Everyone whispered and thought about what it would be like to be that person. (Kathy)

We usually read a story then talked about it for a while and then we wrote about it. . . . I like to talk about books and it's better now. (Rory)

When I'm reading a book . . . most of the time I think about like what they are doing and I'm and sometimes I write it down. (Thomas)

When the teacher is reading it I usually make pictures of it in my mind, and I write about it. (John)

OTHER TEACHERS, SOME YEARS LATER

The way present teachers talk about students who participated in envisionment-building classes in earlier grades gives us a clue that the earlier experiences made an impact. Often they talk about the students as "enjoying literature," having "insights," and "asking questions." Not all the students are academically strong, but their teachers find that they seem excited by books and by talking about them. Some of the students will be familiar from their own comments in the preceding section.

About John, Rory, Thomas, and Kathy, Ms. Ungerski said:

I would say all four of them [who had been in an envisionment-building class 2 years earlier] internalize what they read and ask questions about it more so than other students in the class. In a sense they internalize, they think about it and then they filter through their own lives or their own lives through what they read and discuss. In a sense they truly do make it their own.

Other students might say, "How did he do that or why did he do that?" John would say, "I'll give you an example with Peter and the Wolf. For example, if his grandfather has said don't go out there because of the wolves. Why did Peter not do what the grandfather had said."

Reggie's teacher said:

He seeks out students who ask questions. He's also willing to disagree. When he feels that, he will wait for other children to say something and he'll wait till everyone has gotten the information and then he'll say, "Well, I thought kind of like that, but what I really thought was." And then he'll disagree and kind of take a different turn, a kind of different sense of understanding.

About Greg, Ms. Josephs said:

Greg has good questions, bits of insights. Divergent, what's going to happen, an interesting way of thinking. His comments, I might not have thought of that.

And Ms. Gregg-Greene said about John:

[John's] comments are not mainstream, but they are not way off either. Maybe they are completely different than the way I was looking at the book. He helps other kids reach . . . when he makes a comment, kids are kind of taught to, "agree with so and so, or like so and so said." He helps other kids to do that also when he talks about a book. He has helped other kids to see it from a different point of view.

Ms. Stopper said of Jane:

Jane kind of acts like she's the teacher [laughter]. She'll say to me, like she was reading about historical characters. "Ms. Stopper, would Malie do this? I feel . . . what do you think" [laughter]. In fact, I've grown to read, I happen to like the same type of literature, and maybe she knows that, because I told her I was familiar with some of them. So, when she is reading one, I'll often take one, and go a little, so I can kind of, if she says she is on this chapter of the book, I can say, "Oh." I can reread the same so that we can really have a conversation. She just loves it so much and I enjoy speaking with her. . . . I think many of those students that we did those things with during the past couple of years are engaging others.

All this underscores that literature is a discipline like mathematics and science. It has a content to be learned but also a way of reasoning underlying it. It involves a way of thinking about things and solving problems that is useful not only in the understanding of literature but also in academic learning and daily living—when we are engaged in discourse with others and when we are thinking alone. Although literary reasoning is both creative and imaginative, it is also highly intellectual in a particular kind of way. It has the potential to increase the breadth of reasoning and experience that all students can call upon and use across all avenues of thought and learning, throughout their lives. Who knows what presently unthinkable thoughts they will turn into the realities of tomorrow?

References

Aiken, J. (1988). The rocking donkey. In J. L. Chaparro & M. A. Trose (Eds.), *Reading literature* (pp. 222–227). Evanston, IL: McDougal, Littell. (Original work published 1959)

Applebee, A. (1994). Toward a thoughtful curriculum: Fostering discipline-based conversation. *English Journal, 83*(3), 45–52.

Applebee, A., & Langer, J. A. (1983). Instructional scaffolding: Reading and writing as natural language activities. *Language Arts, 60*(2), 168–175.

Bakhtin, M. (1981). *The dialogic imagination* (C. Emerson & M. Helquist, Trans.). Austin, TX: University of Texas Press.

Barbules, N. C., & Rice, S. (1991). Dialogue across difference: Continuing the conversation. *Harvard Educational Review, 61*(4), 393–416.

Barnes, D. (1976). *From communication to curriculum.* Harmondsworth, England: Penguin Books.

Barthes, R. (1967). *Writing degree zero.* New York: Farrar, Straus & Giroux.

Barthes, R. (1977). *Image, music, text* (S. Heath, Trans.). New York: Hill & Wang.

Barthes, R. (1986). *The rustle of language.* New York: Farrar, Straus & Giroux.

Benton, S. (1992). *Secondary worlds: Literature teaching and the visual arts.* Buckingham, England: Open University Press.

Bereiter, C. (1994). Implications of postmodernism for science, or science as progressive discourse. *Educational Psychologist, 29*(1), 3–12.

Birnbaum, S. (1986). Birth of the moon. *Science World, 43*, 4–6.

Bizzell, P. (1992). *Academic discourse and critical consciousness.* Pittsburgh, PA: University of Pittsburgh Press.

Bizzell, P. (1994). Contact zones and English studies. *College English, 56*(2), 163–169.

Bloome, D., & Egan-Robertson, A. (1993). The social construction of inter-textuality in classroom reading and writing lessons. *Reading Research Quarterly, 28*(4), 304–333.

Booth, W. (1988). *The company we keep: An ethics of fiction.* Berkeley, CA: University of California Press.

Bradbury, R. (1973). I see you never. In A. Purves (Ed.), *Literature education in ten countries* (pp. 340–341). New York: John Wiley.

Bradbury, R. (1992). All summer in a day. In J. N. Beatty & W. L. McBride (Eds.), *Literature and language* (pp. 123–129). Evanston, IL: McDougal, Littell. (Original work published 1954)

Britton, J. (1970). *Language and learning.* London: Penguin Press.

Brown, R. (1958). *Words and things.* New York: Free Press.

Bruner, J. (1986). *Actual minds, possible worlds.* Cambridge, MA: Harvard University Press.

Bruner, J. (1990). *Acts of meaning.* Cambridge, MA: Harvard University Press.

Bruner, J. (1992). The autobiographical process. In R. Folkenflik (Ed.), *The culture of autobiography: Construction of self-representation* (pp. 38–56). Stanford, CA: Stanford University Press.

Calvino, I. (1986). *The uses of literature.* New York: Harcourt Brace Jovanovich.

Cazden, C. (1988). *Classroom discourse.* Portsmouth, NH: Heinemann.

Chayefsky, P. (1983). Marty. In O. S. Niles, E. J. Farrell, & R. M. Leblanc (Eds.), *Album, USA* (pp. 92–119). Glenview, IL: Scott Foresman. (Original work published 1955)

Chopin, K. (1984). The story of an hour. In S. M. Gilbert (Ed.), *The awakening and other selected stories* (pp. 198–200). New York: Penguin.

Coffin, R. P. T. (1939).The secret heart. In *Collected poems of Robert P. Tristram Coffin* (pp. 172–173). New York: Macmillan.

Coffin, R. P. T. (1966). Forgive my guilt. In S. Dunning, E. Lueders, & H. Smith (Eds.), *Reflections on a gift of watermelon pickle* (p. 79). New York: Lothrop, Lee & Shepard. (Original work published 1949)

Cuban, L. (1984). *How teachers taught: Constancy and change in American classrooms 1890–1980.* New York: Longman.

Delpit, L. (1988). The silenced dialogue: Power and psychology in educating other people's children. *Harvard Educational Review, 58,* 280–298.

Derrida, J. (1980). The law of genre. In W. J. T. Mitchell (Ed.), *On Narrative* (pp. 51–78). Chicago: University of Chicago Press.

Dewey, J. (1899). *The school and society.* Chicago: University of Chicago Press.

Dyson, A. (1994). Confronting the split between "the child" and children. *English Education, 26,* 12–28.

Egan, K., & Nadaner, D. (Eds.). (1988). *Imagination and education.* New York: Teachers College Press.

Ellison, R. (1972). *The invisible man.* New York: Vintage Books.

Fillmore, C. J. (1981). Ideal readers and real readers. *Proceedings of the 32nd Georgetown University Round Table Conference.*

Foucault, M. (1981). The order of discourse. In M. Young (Ed.), *Untying the text: A post structuralist reader* (pp. 48–78). London: Routledge & Kegan Paul.

Gates, H. L., Jr. (1992). *Loose canons: Notes on the culture wars.* New York: Oxford University Press.

Goodman, Y. (1985). Kidwatching: Observing young children in the classroom. In A. Jagger & T. Smith-Burke (Eds.), *Observing the language learner* (pp. 9–18). Newark, DE: International Reading Association/National Council of Teachers of English.

Greene, M. (1988). What happened to imagination. In K. Egan & D. Nadaner (Eds.), *Imagination and education* (pp. 45–46). New York: Teachers College Press.

Greene, M. (1993). The passions of pluralism: Multiculturalism and the expanding community. *Educational Researcher, 22*(1), 13–18.

Greene, M. (1995). Art and imagination: Reclaiming the sense of possibility. *Phi Delta Kappan, 76* (5), 378–382.

Grice, H. P. (1975). Logic and conversation. In P. Cole & J. L. Morgan (Eds.), *Syntax and semantics: Vol. 3. Speech acts.* New York: Seminar Press.

Harding, D. W. (1937). The role of the onlooker. *Scrutiny, 6*(3), 247–258.

Harris, J. (1988). Spectator as theorist. *English Education, 20*(1), 41–50.

Heath, S. B. (1983). *Ways with words.* New York: Cambridge University Press.

Iser, W. (1974). *The implied reader: Patterns of communication in prose fiction from Bunyan to Beckett.* Baltimore: Johns Hopkins University Press.

Jackson, S. (1976). Charles. In S. Jackson, *The lottery and other stories* (pp. 91–96). New York: Farrar, Straus & Giroux. (Original work published 1948)

Johnston, P. (1994). *Constructive evaluation of literary engagement.* New York: Longman.

Kay, P. (1987). Three properties of the ideal reader. In R. Freedle & R. Duran (Eds.), *Cognitive and linguistic analyses of test performance* (pp. 208–224). Norwood, NJ: Ablex.

Kelly, G. (1955). *The psychology of personal constructs.* New York: Norton.

Kingsolver, B. (1989). *The bean trees.* New York: HarperCollins.

Langer, J. A. (1984). Literacy instruction in American schools: Problems and perspectives. *American Educational Research Journal, 93*, 107–132.

Langer, J. A. (1985). Levels of questioning: An alternative view. *Reading Research Quarterly, 20*(5), 586–602.

Langer, J. A. (1986). *Children reading and writing: Structures and strategies.* Norwood, NJ: Ablex.

Langer, J. A. (1987a). How readers construct meaning. In R. Freedle (Ed.), *Cognitive and linguistic analyses of standardized test performance* (pp. 225–244). Norwood, NJ: Ablex.

Langer, J. A. (1987b). A sociocognitive perspective on literacy. In J. Langer (Ed.), *Language, literacy, and culture: Issues of society and schooling* (pp. 1–20). Norwood, NJ: Ablex.

Langer, J. A. (1990). The process of understanding: Reading for literary and informational purposes. *Research in the Teaching of English, 24*(3), 229–260.

Langer, J. A. (1992). Discussion as exploration: Literature and the horizon of possibilities. In G. Newell & R. Durst (Eds.), *The role of discussion and writing in the teaching and learning of literature* (pp. 23–24). Norwood, MA: Christopher Gordon Publishers.

Langer, J. A. (1994). Focus on research: A response-based approach to reading literature. *Language Arts, 71*, 203–211.

Langer, J. A. (1995). Literature and learning to think. *Journal of Curriculum and Supervision, 10*(3), 207–226.

Langer, J. A., & Applebee, A. (1986). Reading and writing instruction: Toward a theory of teaching and learning. In E. Rothkopf (Ed.), *Review of research in education* (pp. 171–194). Washington, DC: American Educational Research Association.

Langer, J. A., & Applebee, A. (1987). *How writing shapes thinking.* Urbana, IL: National Council of Teachers of English.

Langer, J. A., Bartolome, L., Lucas, T., & Vasquez, O. (1990). Meaning construction in school literacy tasks: A study of bilingual students. *American Educational Research Journal, 27*(3), 427–471.

Langer, S. (1942). *Philosophy in a new key.* Cambridge, MA: Harvard University Press.

Langer, S. (1967). *Mind: An essay on human feeling.* Baltimore: Johns Hopkins University Press.

Lauter, P. (1990). The literatures of America: A comparative discipline. In A. L. B. Ruoff & J. W. Ward Jr. (Eds.), *Redefining American literary history* (pp. 9–34). New York: Modern Language Association.

Leont'ev, A. N. (1981). The problem of activity in psychology. In J. V. Wertsch (Ed.), *The concept of activity in Soviet psychology* (pp. 37–71). Armonk, NY: Sharpe.

Marshall, J. D. (1989). *Patterns of discourse in classroom discussions of literature* (Report Series 2.9). Albany, NY: Center for the Learning and Teaching of Literature.

Marshall, J. D., Klages, M. B., & Fehlman, R. (1990). *Discussions of literature in lower track classrooms* (Report Series 2.10). Albany, NY: Center for the Learning and Teaching of Literature.

Mayher, J. S. (1990). *Uncommon sense.* Portsmouth, NH: Heinemann.

Minnick, E. (1990). *Transforming knowledge.* Philadelphia: Temple University Press.

Morrison, T. (1974). *Sula.* New York: Knopf.

Morrison, T. (1987). *Beloved.* New York: Knopf.

Naidoo, B. (1986). *Journey to Jo'burg: A South African story.* New York: Harper & Row.

National Assessment of Educational Progress. (1990). *Reading objectives: 1990 assessment.* Princeton, NJ: Educational Testing Service.

National Assessment of Educational Progress. (1992). *Reading framework for the 1992 National Assessment of Educational Progress.* Princeton, NJ: Educational Testing Service.

National Assessment of Educational Progress. (1995). *Reading assessment reconsidered.* Princeton, NJ: Educational Testing Service.

Nervo, A. (1988). I was born today. In J. L. Chaparro & M. A. Tross, *Reading literature* (p. 264). Evanston, IL: McDougal, Littell. (Original work published c. 1900)

Philips, D. (1994). Telling it straight: Issues in assessing narrative research. *Educational Psychologist, 29*(1), 13–22.

Pratt, M. L. (1976). *Toward a speech act theory of literary discourse.* Bloomington, IN: Indiana University Press.

Pratt, M. L. (1991). Arts of the contact zone. *Profession 91*, Modern Language Association, 33–40.

Radway, J. (1984). *Reading the romance: Women, patriarchy, & popular literature.* Chapel Hill, NC: University of North Carolina Press.

Reiss, T. J. (1992). *The meaning of literature.* Ithaca, NY: Cornell University Press.

Ricoeur, P. (1980). On narrative time. In W. J. T. Mitchell (Ed.), *On narrative* (pp. 165–186). Chicago: University of Chicago Press.

Roberts, D., & Langer, J. (1991). *Supporting the process of literary understanding: An analysis of a classroom discussion* (Report Series 2.15). Albany, NY: National Research Center on Literature Teaching and Learning.

Rogoff, B. (1990). *Apprenticeship in thinking.* New York: Oxford University Press.

Rosenblatt, L. (1978). *The reader, the text, the poem.* Cambridge, MA: Harvard University Press.

Santa Barbara Classroom Discourse Group. (1993). [Special issues]. *Linguistics in Education, 5* (3, 4).

Scholes, R. (1985). *Textual power: Literary theory and the teaching of English.* New Haven, CT: Yale University Press.

Scholes, R. (1989). *Protocols of reading.* New Haven, CT: Yale University Press.

Scollon, R., & Scollon, S. K. (1981). *Narrative, literacy, and interethnic communication.* Norwood, NJ: Ablex.

Searle, J. (1969). *Speech acts: An essay on the philosophy of language.* London: Cambridge University Press.

Sophocles. (trans. 1982). *Antigone.* In R. Fagles (Trans.), *Sophocles: The three Theban plays.* New York: Viking Press. (Original work c. 441 B.C.)

Steinbeck, J. (1989). Flight. In *The American Experience* (pp. 172–184). Englewood Cliffs, NJ: Prentice-Hall.

Street, B. (1984). *Literacy in theory and practice.* New York: Cambridge University Press.

Tolstoy, L. (1984). The king and the shirt. In *Junior great books: Fables* (pp. 39–43). Chicago: Great Books Foundation. (Original work published c. 1866)

Van Allsburg, C. (1990). *Just a dream.* New York: Houghton Mifflin.

Vygotsky, L. S. (1962). *Thought and language.* Cambridge, MA: Harvard University Press.

Wagner, D. (1991). Literacy and culture: Emic and etic perspectives. In T. Jennings & A. Purves (Eds.), *Literate systems and individual lives: Perspectives on literacy and schooling* (pp. 11–22). Albany, NY: State University of New York Press.

Walker, A. (1990). The abortion. In W. Martin (Ed.), *We are the stories we tell: The best short stories by North American women since 1945* (pp. 207–217). New York: Pantheon Books.

Walker, A. (1992). *Possessing the secret of joy.* New York: Harcourt Brace Jovanovich.

Walmsley, S. (1994). *Children exploring their worlds.* Portsmouth, NH: Heinemann.

Walmsley, S., & Walp, T. (1989). *Teaching literature in the elementary school* (Report Series 1.3). Albany, NY: Center for the Learning and Teaching of Literature.

Warnock, M. (1976). *Imagination.* London: Faber & Faber.

Weir, R. (1962). *Language in the crib.* The Hague: Mouton & Co.

Wells, G., & Chang-Wells, G. L. (1992). *Constructing knowledge together*. Portsmouth, NH: Heinemann.

Wertsch, J. V. (1991). *Voices of the mind*. Cambridge, MA: Harvard University Press.

Willinsky, J. (1991). *The triumph of literature: The fate of literacy: English in the secondary school curriculum*. New York: Teachers College Press.

Witherell, C., & Noddings, N. (Eds.). (1991). *We are the stories we tell*. New York: Teachers College Press.

Wolf, S., & Heath, S. B. (1993). *The braid of literature*. Cambridge, MA: Harvard University Press.

Yolen, J. (1990). *Sky dogs*. San Diego, CA: Harcourt Brace Jovanovich.

Yolen, J. (1991). *Greyling*. New York: Putnam.

Index

About the Author

Judith A. Langer is Professor of Education at the State University of New York at Albany. She specializes in literacy and education. Her major works focus on how people become highly literate, on how they use reading and writing to learn, and on what this means for instruction. She uses her research to inform the development of more effective theories of literacy instruction and achieve improved learning for all students.

Langer has published widely. Some of her books include *Children Reading and Writing: Structures and Strategies*; *Language, Literacy, and Culture: Issues of Society and Schooling*; *How Writing Shapes Thinking: Studies of Teaching and Learning*; *Literature Instruction: A Focus on Student Response*; and *Literature Instruction: Practice and Policy*.

Langer is codirector of the National Research Center on Literature Teaching and Learning, funded by the U.S. Department of Education, Office of Educational Research and Improvement. She is senior scholar at the Writing and Literacy Center, SUNY Albany.